CLOSE PROTECTION – THE SOFTER SKILLS

Geoffrey Padgham

ENTERTAINMENT TECHNOLOGY PRESS

Security Series

CLOSE PROTECTION – THE SOFTER SKILLS

Geoffrey Padgham

Entertainment Technology Press

Close Protection – The Softer Skills

© Geoffrey Padgham
Illustrations © Bill Mevin
Cover photographs © EMPICS

First edition published September 2006
by Entertainment Technology Press Ltd
The Studio, High Green, Great Shelford, Cambridge CB22 5EG
Internet: www.etnow.com

ISBN 1 904031 39 0

A title within the
Entertainment Technology Press Security Series
Series editor: John Offord
in association with Buckinghamshire New University

All rights reserved. No part of this publication may be reproduced in any material form (including photocopying or storing in any medium by electronic means and whether or not transiently or incidentally to some other use of this publication) without the written permission of the copyright holder except in accordance with the provisions of the Copyright, Designs and Patents Act 1988. Applications for the copyright holder's written permission to reproduce any part of this publication should be addressed to the publishers.

The contents of this publication are provided in good faith and neither The Author nor The Publisher can be held responsible for any errors or omissions contained herein. Any person relying upon the information must independently satisfy himself or herself as to the safety or any other implications of acting upon such information and no liability shall be accepted either by The Author or The Publisher in the event of reliance upon such information nor for any damage or injury arising from any interpretation of its contents. This publication may not be used as any part of a risk assessment.

CODE / CP004-0907

CONTENTS

THE AUTHOR

I was born in Dartford, Kent on the 16th of October 1952, the third son of Gertrude Phyllis Mary and Wilfred Horace Padgham. My main childhood friends were two brothers David and Jeremy Morton. I was tall for my age, and David was both shorter and slighter. His stature made him a regular target for the school bullies, so it quite naturally followed that I became his protector. You could say that this was my first experience of Close Protection (CP)!

From about five years of age it had always been my desire to become a police officer, and join the world-famous Metropolitan Police in London. So at the age of sixteen, I applied to join the Metropolitan Police Cadet Corps (MPCC) based at Hendon in north London. The MPCC was a youth scheme to fill the gap between school leaving age and joining the Metropolitan Police as a Constable at the youngest possible age of nineteen.

After a successful application and interview I was accepted into the MPCC on 28th April 1969. The MPCC programme of activities at both Hendon and Ashford Cadet Schools was extensive, and I decided to try my hand at just about everything. Apart from the mandatory core educational studies and limited police instruction, the emphasis was on sporting activities. I took part in rugby, judo, wrestling, rope climbing, abseiling, athletics, basketball, canoeing and anything else on offer. I excelled in some sports, got by in others, but truly embraced the philosophy of "It is not the winning that's the only important part of sport, but also just the taking part!"

On 18th October 1971 I joined the Metropolitan Police as a recruit Constable and completed four months initial training at Hendon Police Training College. On completion I transferred to Marylebone Lane Police Station in Central London. There I spent five very busy years followed by promotion to Sergeant and a transfer to Peckham Police Station in South East London.

In August 1979, Irish Terrorists tragically murdered Earl Mountbatten of Burma, and applications for new Royalty Close Protection Officers (CPOs) were invited. Shortly afterwards I attended a formal selection interview at New Scotland Yard, and having been successful I joined Royalty Protection's A1 Branch on Monday 10th September 1979. As a young 26 year-old sergeant based at Buckingham Palace, I had to adjust quickly and come to terms with my new responsibilities as a 'Back Up' sergeant. Provision of close protection to Her Majesty The Queen and all other members of the British Royal family was under intense scrutiny. There was much pressure on everyone in the

Branch to provide a discreet, but effective close protection service and yet always 'get it right'.

With a small team of back-up Sergeants providing close protection support to the whole of the royal family, you can just imagine how busy we all were. I spent much of my time away from home, driving a back-up car from one end of the United Kingdom to the other. In mid-1982 a career opportunity developed for me and I was asked to transfer from support close protection, to become one of only two Personal Protection Officers (PPOs) with His Royal Highness The Prince Andrew. I was delighted to be asked to undertake this role with the second son of Her Majesty The Queen, particularly as it had always been my preference to work with a younger member of the Royal family. This new appointment saw me promoted to the rank of Acting Inspector, later made substantive in 1986, and assume the role of deputy team leader. At this particular time Sub Lieutenant His Royal Highness The Prince Andrew was on active service with the Royal Navy, as a Sea-King helicopter pilot embarked in HMS Invincible during the Falklands War. He returned from the South Atlantic in September 1982, and my first official period of personal protection duty commenced at Balmoral Castle in Scotland.

After a whirlwind familiarisation of the Balmoral Estate and hardly any time to settle into the new job, my first foreign trip took place in October 1982. In my capacity as a PPO I accompanied Prince Andrew, Koo Stark and other holiday guests to the Caribbean holiday island of Mustique. On the outward-bound British Airways flight to Barbados, a piece of bad luck occurred when a British tabloid newspaper photographer travelling privately on holiday recognised both Prince Andrew and Ms Stark on the aircraft. I obviously realised that word of the private holiday was about to become public knowledge, and that the world's tabloid press and international paparazzi would quickly descend on Mustique. The trip rapidly turned into what could best be described as my close protection 'baptism by fire'. In hindsight, it proved to be a catalyst in establishing my close professional relationship with Prince Andrew. A trust and chemistry developed between us, and I remained in the same job for the next seventeen years. I travelled the world very extensively, and ultimately worked with every member of the royal family in some capacity or another.

A highlight of my police and royal service was in 1991 when I was made a Member of the Royal Victorian Order (MVO), which is a personal award from Her Majesty The Queen.

Throughout the late 1980's and early 1990's even though I had received no formal training as an instructor, I supported CP training in many different ways. In the mid 1990's Royalty Protection reviewed its selection processes and it later became linked to a broader training review encompassing every element of police 'Bodyguard Training'. In 1997 a new training regime was being developed, with opportunities for existing experienced protection officers to be trained as trainers. This approach greatly appealed to my passion for quality training, and in early 1998 I attended a 'train the trainers' course specifically designed for experienced protection officers. In June 1998 I was approached to take up a new appointment as one of the Inspectors in charge of the Close Protection Team at Buckingham Palace. This post would give me specific responsibilities for Royalty CPO selection, the new modular CP training course and the skills development of all new Royalty Protection Officers. The timing of this offer and the unique opportunity to be instrumental in further developing the CP course, was an opportunity I could not allow to pass by.

To voluntarily leave my current post after nearly two decades working with Prince Andrew was a very difficult decision to make. I felt strongly that I alone should raise the issue with His Royal Highness and have an opportunity to fully discuss my decision to leave his household. In November 1998 I spoke to Prince Andrew privately and informed him of my decision to leave for my new appointment. I was greatly encouraged by his wholehearted support for my career move into Operations and CP training. I took up my new appointment in April 1999.

The next three years saw me heavily involved in managing the CPO team at Buckingham Palace, with much emphasis placed on the new protection training course and officers' personal development. As part of my vision for protection officers' Continuing Professional Development (CPD), I sought the assistance of one of my team members, Sergeant Philip Clements. As my training sergeant he was a highly qualified trainer and together we developed a coaching and mentoring scheme for new protection officers. The scheme followed on from a CPO's initial training, through his or her first twelve months on Royalty Protection duty. It was designed to increase the involvement of experienced protection officers in the training process and tap into their huge knowledge and expertise as 'on-the-job' coaches. Like all new programmes, it had its teething problems, but the process gained momentum and general support purely by involving as many people in the process as possible.

With a feeling of contentment and most management systems and training processes in place, I retired from Royalty Protection and the Metropolitan

Police Service (MPS) on an ordinary pension on the 18th November 2001.

After retirement I commenced work as a Liaison Officer for the United Kingdom (UK) Foreign and Commonwealth Office, and an event manager working in partnership with Malcolm Godfrey, a former Royal Navy officer who is the proprietor of 'Time For Greenwich'. In addition I slowly established myself in the private security industry as a specialist CP training consultant and instructor.

In early 2004 the Security Industry Authority (SIA), as the regulator for the private security industry, started consultation to develop a qualification for the licensing of private close protection personnel. As a subject expert, I joined the SIA Close Protection Consultation Group for training and qualifications. After much work by many people I am delighted to say that the final specification for core competency training and qualifications for CPOs fully reflects the softer skills of close protection that I wholeheartedly support. At the time of writing this book and as a co-founding Director of Anubis Associates Limited (AAL), a private security company, I am teaching those skills as a principal instructor and consultant on various Close Protection Training Courses.

In 2005 I became a member of the Protective Security Management Foundation Degree Steering Committee of Buckinghamshire Chilterns University College (BCUC) in High Wycombe. I am pleased to be a member of

MEVIN

A portrait of the Author

a group developing the close protection foundation degree course, and am confident that it will further promote best practice and a growing professionalism within the CP sector.

I have been blessed with a wonderful marriage to Sue, my wife of the last twenty-six years. She has given much to me, the service, and ultimately our home and family with two fantastic sons David and Alan. One of the disadvantages of a long career in close protection, are the many necessary, but regular absences from loved ones and the resultant loss of family time. It was a necessary evil of the job, but at least I am now making up for it!

It is extremely rewarding to have completed such an interesting and challenging career in the Metropolitan Police, particularly my specialisation in close protection duties. If you add to this my role in the development and training delivery of close protection in both the police and private sector, I believe it placed me in a unique position to write this educational book.

Geoffrey Padgham MVO

THE ILLUSTRATOR

Bill Mevin studied at Liverpool School of Art before joining Gaumont British Studios as a trainee film animator under the auspices of David Hand (top Disney Director of Snow White and Bambi). David appointed Bill character designer, and this led to animation work on the first British full-length cartoon film 'Animal Farm' and various shorts.

Later he entered the world of children's comics, and for several years drew many well-known TV characters including Dr Who, Popeye, Bugs Bunny, Yogi Bear, Bill and Ben, The Morphs, Space Patrol and many more. He then created a cartoon strip satirizing the American television soaps Dallas and Dynasty, which was bought by the Daily Mail and was given the star treatment under the title of 'The Soapremes'.

Since 1992 Bill has been drawing the world-famous cartoon strip 'The Perishers', which, until recently, was a regular cartoon strip in a UK national newspaper the *Daily Mirror* for almost fifty years.

A self-portrait of the Illustrator

ACKNOWLEDGEMENTS

My first thanks must go to my parents whose support throughout my early years and in joining the Metropolitan Police was immense. Without their encouragement I would have been unlikely to follow a path that has ultimately enabled me to write this book. Secondly to my life-long friend Steve Stokes who has helped me in countless ways from our meeting as Metropolitan Police Cadets in 1971, right through three decades to recently proof-reading this book. He has always been there to give me his honest advice and support – a huge thank you!

Although my time on uniform duty in the Metropolitan Police was a happy one, Royalty Protection was the period that established my knowledge base and experiences to write this book. Many people were integral to my evolving protection career path, but none more so than Commander Michael Trestrail who selected me in the first place.

For 17 years HRH The Prince Andrew (now HRH The Duke of York) was very supportive of my position as his Personal Protection Officer (PPO).

This period embedded a huge amount of knowledge about close protection, and our professional working relationship was something I shall always cherish and remember with fondness – Thank you Sir!

Also thanks to the countless people I met and worked with during my long association with the Royal Navy (RN). From attachments to the Royal Naval Air Stations at Culdrose, Portland and Yeovilton to serving alongside crews in HMS Invincible, HMS Brazen and other RN ships. I had an enviable role by being allowed all the privileges of an officer in the Wardroom, without having the need to go to sea. I have particularly fond memories of working with Lieutenant Commander Rory McLean who was the First Lieutenant in HMS Brazen during my time there from 1984 to 1986. It was a tough job being the 'Runs Ashore Officer' but someone had to do it!

I owe a great debt of gratitude to my principal partner in HRH The Duke of York's household, Chief Inspector Stephen Burgess, who helped me both at the selection stage and later during my formative years as a PPO. Also to Captain Neil Blair, Private Secretary to HRH The Duke of York with whom I shared many working days both in the UK and abroad. His friendship, professionalism and firm approach to planning during many a trip completely confirmed my view that time spent on reconnaissance was never wasted.

In 1998 I undertook a 'Train the Trainers' course under the leadership of Sergeant Philip Clements, which was a revelation in my police career. It completed an unfinished training process jigsaw puzzle, and provided me with the knowledge and professional tools to be fully prepared to manage Close Protection training ever since. I had always been interested and supported close protection training issues and initiatives, but this course was a defining moment that ultimately changed my career path.

Chief Inspector John Askew, a friend and work colleague since 1972, encouraged and supported me in many different ways, but he was particularly instrumental in my appointment as the Royalty Protection Training Inspector.

Bill Mevin is my friend, neighbour and multi-talented artist, who through his enclosed illustrations has perfectly captured the correct mix of professionalism and humour in close protection. Just like the job itself really!

It would be impossible to mention every member of the various Royal Households, police-staff, colleagues and friends who have helped me in some way or another over the years. Suffice it to say that I am eternally grateful for your support and friendship, and I apologise for not mentioning you by name.

Last but definitely not least my love and sincere thanks go especially to my wife Susan who was, and I am delighted to say still is, always there for me. Despite long hours and my many periods away from home, her devotion and support as wife, friend and mother to our children was immense. My love and thanks also go to my two sons David and Alan, who have developed into fine young men with their own unique modern approach and style. A special thank you for spending time helping with this book, and providing many suggestions and objective comments to improve it. Thanks for understanding and apologies for the absences, but I hope I have now been able to make up some of the lost time! I love you all.

Geoffrey Padgham MVO, Bromley, Kent
September 2006

INTRODUCTION

From the outset it is worth stating that unlike many other books on protection, this is not a collection of sexy 'bodyguard' stories designed to seduce you by using and abusing the force of hard skills. If you are seeking a 'dish-the-dirt' read about the British Royal Family or a behind the scenes insight into life at Buckingham Palace, then I suggest you look elsewhere! This publication is designed to be educational, strikes at the reality of CP in the western world, and will provide you with some basic but realistic guidelines for employment in the private close protection sector.

Where I express gender throughout the book, I have decided to use the pronoun 'he' rather than constantly refer to 'he' and 'she'. This decision will enhance the book's readability, and is not meant as any offence to the female reader or the many professional female operators in the Close Protection sector.

Close Protection is more widely known by the general public as the role undertaken by people calling themselves Bodyguards. It often conjures up the image of a tall, large-framed man sporting dark glasses and looking menacing much like the character 'Odd Job' in the James Bond film 'Goldfinger'. There will always be a place in the Private Security Industry (PSI) for people who fit this description, but more often than not they are employed by wealthy celebrities who are more interested in drawing attention to themselves rather than avoiding it. The presence of a large and frightening individual as a fashion accessory to the rich and famous can act as a good deterrent to the over-enthusiastic fan, but it will not necessarily deter the mentally ill, a stalker or a committed criminal. The old-fashioned bodyguard's role tended to consist of just being a presence, and generally lacked a degree of pro-active thinking to prevent potential problems from developing. This simplistic approach to close protection is therefore geared to reacting to threats and difficulties, rather than preventing them from occurring in the first place.

Most books on protection over-emphasise the word bodyguard and focus on the sensationalised elements of the role. They give the impression that criminals and terrorists lurk on every corner, constantly placing a protected person (*Principal*) at an extremely high level of risk. A common misconception of the skills required for CP is that you need to be armed to the teeth, possess the ability to drive like a professional rally driver, have the stature of Mr.Universe or have a black belt in some form of martial arts. I specifically describe these skills as some of the harder elements of protection. Proficiency in the use of firearms is an excellent example of a harder CP skill regularly trained by the police, military and civilian personnel. In many respects carrying a firearm is viewed as a pre-requisite to be an effective CPO. However, history has shown that statistically the reality is that during an attack on a protected person, they are very rarely used as a means of defence. Although carrying a firearm can be integral and useful for the role, particularly in hostile environments, in most areas of commercial close protection in the western world they are unnecessary and illegal.

Being physically fit for the role, and highly trained in immediate first aid care, are good examples of harder skills that are much more necessary for CP. In many respects fitness fully prepares you for the long hours experienced in operational protection and will enable you to react quickly in the event of an incident. First aid is probably the most used skill on a regular basis, whether dealing with a cut finger or a principal's suspected heart attack. Therefore, without dismissing the need for training in some of the harder skill areas, this book will specifically concentrate on a CPO's need to master the softer skills and in particular the very important art of communication. It can be argued that effective use of communication and the other softer skills will often negate the need to use some of the harder skills. By making the above comments I have not lost any focus of the CP role, but have tried to take a realistic approach and rationalise reality from fiction.

More than any other competency I passionately believe that effective communication is the key softer skill for CP. It constantly touches all our lives from mediated forms such as letters and e-mail, to the personal elements of face-to-face interpersonal skills. The first time you set eyes on someone, you are sending and receiving non-verbal communication signals long before you engage in conversation. The professional working relationship with the protected person should be a top-priority for anyone on day one of a Close Protection assignment. It is often achieved by being a personable and likeable individual who is well trained, confident, reliable and efficient. It helps enormously if you are reasonably well-read, and can converse with people from all walks of life. Professional training and a good general knowledge will enable you to talk to the principal and everyone around them with confidence and ease. It matters not how well trained you are in the harder elements of CP, as first impressions and communication skills will initially be the only thing the principal will be interested in. Put simply, if you do not fit into the principal's 'world' or he dislikes you from the outset, you will not be in his employment for long! Therefore, the professional working relationship between a principal and their protection operative is the most important element of the job, but it can also be one of the most difficult to establish. There are many pressures affecting the development of this relationship, from the demands of a principal's family and friends, to dilemmas that can create a 'no win' scenario.

During the twenty-two years that I worked as a Royalty Protection Officer I have always said that there are basically only three types of close protection personnel. There are always exceptions to the rule, but the three types of CP operatives are as follows:

- Thugs
- Average
- Professional

The *Thugs* are very often large mean-looking people who have received little or no formal close protection training. They tend to wear black boots in preference to shoes, completely shave their heads and favour dressing in all-black clothing - much like a funeral assistant. Their sole intention in providing protection is to look menacing, frighten everyone away from the principal, and if necessary push, shove or punch their way out of trouble. Interpersonal communications skills are neither their strongest point nor a first-choice tool in their CP kit bag (if they have one at all).

Average CPOs are generally people who have received limited protection training, and are often 'dominated' individuals more inclined to be a servant than provide a proper close protection service. They willingly undertake many roles unrelated to protection with no clear focus of their core responsibilities. In fact they often have no idea how to provide appropriate protective cover or what 'managing risk' actually involves. When faced with a predicament, *Average* CPOs regularly select the easy option, letting a difficult situation pass without appropriate comment or response, hoping that nothing will happen. I call this the fingers-crossed approach that is generally followed by an eventual sigh of relief and a comment such as 'Got away with that one'.

Professional CPOs are reasonably fit, formally trained, pro-active individuals who have particularly mastered the art of communication and the broader softer skills. They are constantly thinking ahead of the principal and planning potential problems out of the close protection equation. They know when to objectively challenge the protected person, providing good reasons for their decisions when necessary. Generally they are not afraid to stand up and be counted, and tackle difficult issues, often risking the displeasure of the principal. They employ a firm but fair approach. If this group of CPOs had a motto it could be described identically to the personal principles of conflict management: 'awareness, anticipation and avoidance'.

I have now 'set the scene' for the rest of the book. You can identify that a successful CPO is more likely to be a professionally trained pro-active individual who blends into the background and remains unnoticed in a principal's company. Many protected persons, particularly royalty and senior executives want, and will generally accept the presence of a CPO, but will also wish to continue to lead as normal a life as possible. To fit into this environment the thinking protection operative will remain flexible, creating space around the principal whenever possible, and is mindful of the threat, risk, circumstances of an event and in particular the protected person's wishes. It is not an easy balance to achieve, but sound judgement based on these and a range of other factors will ultimately determine the correct approach to constantly managing the close protection risk.

1 THE MYTH OF HARD SKILLS

Most people believe in some kind of myth, whether it is the existence of the Minotaur or that you lose weight in a sauna. These myths also seem to have what we consider to be 'proof' that they are actually true, such as photographs of a strange creature or some pleasing scale readings.

Close Protection is surrounded by its own myth. The media has creatively etched the image of, to use an outdated term, the 'Bodyguard' in the public's minds. Films, television shows and fictional protection stories flood our everyday lives. The general public believe that a 'bodyguard' is a crack shot and karate master, who dodges bullets and evades hordes of attackers whilst two-wheeling a limousine around corners. Sometimes, even the protected person is seduced by the image of CP providing them with a feeling of unwarranted importance.

The origins of this myth come from the unfounded belief that in order to be an effective CPO you need to have mastered the art of protection's hard skills. A further myth is that they will be used inexhaustibly in your battle to keep the principal from harm. Some of these skills are extremely important: particularly fitness, first aid or advanced driver training – and all must be part of your professional repertoire.

Where the confusion often arises is the frequency with which these hard skills are actually put into practice. If you are working in a hostile environment, such as Iraq or some South American countries, then quite naturally the threat and risk to your principal is much higher. In this type of environment you are more likely to encounter a real life-threatening situation, which will require a hard and effective CP response. In the UK however, the threat is quite naturally much lower and a softer approach is often, if not always, a more appropriate and effective method to adopt.

Before I start to outline some examples that, in my mind, support that statement, we should first define the different types of skills that I am referring to:

The 'Hard Skills' include:

- Martial Arts
- Firearms

- Evasive Driving
- Self Defence
- First Aid
- Physical Fitness

The 'Softer Skills' include:

- Communication (interpersonal, assertiveness, written, verbal, diplomatic)
- Listening Ability
- Flexibility
- Quick Thinking
- Negotiating Ability
- Planning Ability
- Organisational Ability
- Professional Standards (honesty, integrity, smartness, punctuality, conscientiousness)
- Teamwork
- Leadership Ability
- Decision Making
- Discretion
- Temperament
- Enthusiasm
- Reliability

These are not inexhaustible lists, so do not believe that all the skills you require to be an effective CPO are listed within these bullet points. Examples of each side of the protection coin show the clear difference between 'Hard Skills' and the 'Softer Skills'. However, without both sides there would not be a coin, so they are both needed, but at different times and in different situations.

'Softer skills' are more professionally titled competencies, and are person-based qualities such as knowledge, skills, attitudes and personal behaviour. These factors are often something you develop throughout the course of your life and are general skills transferable from job to job. The best examples of these qualities are an individual's interpersonal skills or their ability to produce a comprehensive plan. 'Hard skills' generally represent some sort of 'doing' or are reliant on a physical action; something that can be taught from scratch at any age. They are not competencies but are often other specific role-related skills that a person can develop through training and practice.

Having now described the difference between hard and softer skills, you can quickly identify that the softer skills are much more likely to be used on a daily basis. Hard skills are not! Why is it then that some amateur training providers or the media disproportionately emphasise the importance of the hard skills? The answer is simple. It is because they are the more sexy elements of close protection duty. Sensationalising CP 'talks up' the role and attempts to make it more exciting or appealing to the reader. Many 'bodyguard magazines' show photographs of 'so called' CP personnel wearing gas masks and body armour whilst carrying CS spray, smoke canisters and an array of firearms. The carriage of this sort of equipment, except in the most extreme of hostile environments could not be further from the truth!

The most obvious myth-busting example of this is the portrayal, through the media, of firearms or defensive weapons at the core of every close protection operation. Without getting into the technicalities of legislation, current British law makes it illegal for a private citizen to own or carry any sort of firearm in the UK. The carriage of offensive weapons, even for defensive use, is prohibited under several pieces of legislation but particularly Section 1 of the Prevention of Crime Act 1953. This states that "Any person who without lawful authority or reasonable excuse, the proof whereof shall lie on him, has with him in any public place any offensive weapon shall be guilty of an offence". Therefore it can be seen that a private security industry CPO operating in England and Wales cannot legally carry either a firearm or any type of weapon (defensive or otherwise).

This is not to say that many of the 'Hard Skills' of CP are obsolete; they are merely a much smaller percentage of the kit bag tools than the general public realises. For example, it is vitally important that a CPO is highly trained in 'job specific' first aid, so that he can deal with a worst case scenario. Where there has been a successful attack on the principal, a CPO must be adequately trained to provide immediate first aid treatment to any injuries inflicted. Additionally, on a day-to-day basis you must be able to identify the warning signs and provide the proper treatment for illnesses such as diabetes, asthma or a suspected stroke. Physical fitness is necessary for health, alertness and speed of reaction as well as the more obvious physical demands of long hours or conflict management. Driving is arguably a key area to master - but not the

Get down!

specifics of ramming vehicles or high-speed turns, which are fun to practice and of fairly limited use. More mastering the safe, smooth and systematic approach to progressive advanced driving techniques. You will secure more CP employment with an advanced driving qualification than one that states you attended an anti-hijack driving course.

Think Point: "Excluding hostile environments, do you know anyone employed in CP who has ever rammed a vehicle or used violent evasive driving tactics in the western world?" I certainly don't!

So, to put all my comments into perspective, I acknowledge that 'Hard Skills' do have a place in CP training. However, with the exception of fitness, first aid and advanced driver training they are specialist tools that statistically are rarely used. In contrast to this statement, 'Softer Skills' are undoubtedly the most commonly used tools throughout CP assignments, particularly in UK CP.

Myth v Reality

The myth of the real benefits of hard skills is not supported by the facts surrounding past close protection incidents. They obviously have a place in close protection training, but must be put into context with their practical application in the role. In order to separate the myth from the reality of CP events, I will briefly outline three of the key close protection incidents that occurred in 1981:

President Ronald Reagan

On 30th March 1981 the United States President Ronald Reagan was leaving the Hilton Hotel in Washington DC, USA. At 2.26pm the President, surrounded by heavily armed Secret Service Agents and other police officers, walked from the hotel to his motorcade lined-up outside. As President Reagan approached his armoured limousine, hidden within a group of waiting media and well wishers was John Hinckley. Just before the President reached his vehicle, Hinckley fired and unloaded his six-shot revolver at the President. It took just 1.8 seconds for him to fire all six shots, and consequently in that incredibly short period of time no police officer or agent returned any fire.

In the ensuing chaos an array of semi-automatic weapons, revolvers and machine guns appeared from under jackets and out of briefcases. By this time it was all too late. Hinckley had emptied his gun, been jumped upon and was already being restrained by law enforcement agents. Tragically, bullets fired from Hinckley's gun had hit four people including President Reagan. He was struck by a single bullet in the chest that ironically had been deflected from the armoured limousine specifically provided to protect him. Great credit must be given to Special Agent Jerry Parr and the other US Secret Service agents for their speed of reaction to provide body cover to President Reagan and evacuate him from the incident so quickly.

However, the issue I wish to highlight is that despite the presence of all the assembled firepower of the US Secret Service and other local police officers, they were all unable to draw their personal weapons and resort to a firearm as a means of defence. In only 1.8 seconds you do not have enough time to see a weapon, respond to the threat, draw a firearm and shoot back. What actually transpired was a natural human reaction to danger much akin to a street brawl where an attacker is jumped upon and wrestled to the ground. The security forces present had no time to calmly think of a rational response, they just instantly reacted to what they saw.

Her Majesty The Queen

On 13th June 1981 Her Majesty The Queen was riding her horse Burmese to her official birthday celebrations of the Trooping of The Colour ceremony held on Horse Guards Parade in London. As Her Majesty was riding from The Mall into Horse Guards Road, hidden on the corner of the junction within the watching crowd was Marcus Sarjeant. He drew a concealed weapon and fired several shots at The Queen, but with Sarjeant's position concealed within a crowd of innocent members of the public an armed police officer would be extremely unlikely to shoot into that environment. There were armed officers in the immediate vicinity, but once-again the sheer speed of the incident did not allow officers to even consider returning fire. The final result was that Sarjeant was restrained, wrestled to the ground and arrested. This was a similar incident to the attempted assassination of President Reagan, but the main difference was that Sarjeant's weapon was later identified as a starting pistol. No one present at the time of the incident would have been able to instantly identify the difference between a real firearm and a starting pistol - therefore the immediate security response could still have been the same.

President Anwar Sadat

On 6th October 1981 President Anwar Sadat of Egypt was attending the eighth anniversary of the Yom Kippur war with Israel. He was positioned centrally in the Presidential box and was present in his capacity as Field Marshal of the armed forces. Whilst watching a flying display performed by the Egyptian Air Force, a military truck pulled up in front of the presidential reviewing stand and gunmen leapt from the back of the vehicle. They ran towards the Presidential box throwing grenades and firing automatic weapons at President Sadat and the other assembled guests. Despite the presence of large numbers of military and close protection personnel, eyewitnesses stated that the attackers were able to keep shooting for well over a minute. Security personnel eventually returned fire killing two of the gunmen and overpowering the rest. President Sadat was airlifted by helicopter to a military hospital but tragically later died of his injuries.

You will note that all the above attacks involved weapons that could legally justify an armed response from security personnel. Only the assassination of President Sadat resulted in firearms being used as a means of defence, and amongst all the confusion it would appear that the response took quite some time to materialise. All these incidents also occurred at high-risk times, such as the principal being present, leaving or returning from a public event. In each scenario there were highly trained security personnel present around the principal, but action is quicker than re-action and they were given no real opportunity to effectively use their harder skills training.

As you will learn later in the book (Chapter 2), the planned programme, protocol and the wishes of the principal play a major part in CP, often working contrary to the wishes of security. Hindsight is a wonderful thing, but it may be that some of these and other incidents could have been prevented or lessened by the pro-active use of many softer skills (i.e. talking to people in the crowds, planning out problems, adjusting the programme, arriving at a different entrance, screening guests, etc).

Statistically, most close protection incidents involving firearms or otherwise, are all over in a few seconds. This *fact* highlights the extreme difficulties faced by CP teams, particularly those with few personnel and limited resources. Even if you are the best-trained CPO in the world, an expert in both the softer and hard skills, you must remember that *action* is always quicker than *reaction*. Realistically in CP you will rarely get the chance to utilise any of your harder skills training. The emphasis of the modern, professionally trained CPO is to be a forward thinking pro-active person who is one-step ahead of the game!

SIA Specification For CP Training and Qualifications

The SIA Specification for Core Competency Training and Qualifications for the Close Protection Operatives in England and Wales (November 2004), accurately reflects the need to embrace many of the softer skills into CP training. Below is a list of the fifteen mandatory sessions of knowledge and practical skills, required to be covered when undertaking the new minimum 150 guided learning hours SIA Licence CP Course:

- Introduction to the Roles and Responsibilities of the Close Protection Operative
- Threat and Risk Assessment
- Surveillance Awareness
- Operational Planning
- Law and Legislation
- Interpersonal Skills
- Close Protection Teamwork
- Reconnaissance
- Close Protection Foot Techniques
- Route Selection
- Use of Close Protection Vehicle Techniques
- Search Awareness
- Incidents and Dilemmas
- Venue Based Security
- Communication and Conflict Management Skills

You will note that in the Specification above there is no mention of firearms training, evasive driver techniques or martial arts requirements. A large percentage of the qualification syllabus focuses on planning, organisational skills, risk management, teamwork and interpersonal communication skills. Communication is a theme that runs through all elements of CP training, even the hard skills. It is the first port of call in conflict management, is integral to establishing history or symptoms for first aid treatment and is littered across all other mandatory knowledge areas. Some of the most useful softer skills are pro-active avoidance or preventative measures. Adoption of anti and counter surveillance techniques are excellent examples of pro-active CP work specifically employed to prevent and detect unwanted attention on your principal. By starving obsessive followers or potential attackers of their much-needed information about your principal, you will disrupt their intelligence cycle to discourage them enough to seek out an alternative and easier target.

At the end of the day close protection is all about managing risk. In any threat and risk assessment a *lack* of intelligence data or evidence to support any real perceived danger to the principal must also be acknowledged and acted upon. A rigid, reactive, or numbers approach to CP is often a mistake. The attempted assassination of President Reagan highlighted that sheer numbers of security personnel and reactive firepower present at the time of an attack is neither a deterrent nor necessarily the solution. In the private security industry you are highly unlikely to ever have access to the resources made available to many of the official government agencies around the world. Most of the time you will be working on your own or maybe with a maximum of two other people. These people could be trained CPOs or maybe a combination of drivers, secretaries or general staff.

In order to counter this severe lack of resources, I strongly encourage you to give serious thought to fully embracing the softer skills approach of CP detailed throughout the remainder of this book. Whenever possible you must work tirelessly to avoid a potentially embarrassing, ugly or more sinister scenario altogether. I accept that many aspects of close protection are dependant on resources and the principal being both helpful and supportive. However, with an intelligent pro-active approach you will at least be content with the fact that you did everything possible to ensure the continuing safety and well being of your principal.

2 100% SAFE

The primary objective of all personnel employed to provide Close Protection is defined as follows -

"To establish and maintain a safe working environment in which a principal can live and work whilst continually minimising risk"

Security Industry Authority 2004

The SIA definition of close protection above begs someone to ask the question; "In these circumstances what does the word *safe* really mean?" The obvious response is to protect the principal from attack, but in close protection there are other wider issues that are equally important such as image, profile or embarrassment. The latter can often be more important to the principal than the former! CP is not an exact science and can best be described as the practical application of skills to produce an appropriate response to a close protection task. It is not about the use of rigid drills generally favoured by the military, nor about inflexible contingency plans. The role requires a Close Protection Operative to be alert to evolving events, and be able to adopt a flexible response to incidents and emergencies.

This Chapter is not designed to enlighten you with an in-depth analysis of *'Threat'* and *'Risk'*, which can be a combination of factors to provide you with a mathematical solution on a sliding scale. It will however provide you with a fundamental understanding of assessing the main threats, which are often issues of the principal's health and lifestyle rather than kidnappers or terrorist activity. In order to fully grasp this Chapter you need to know the different groups of people who receive close protection, and how they can often compromise the practical provision of CP.

Protected Persons

In the vast majority of cases an individual will start to receive close protection as a direct result of career success, high political office, wealth, a position of birth or a real perceived threat against them. Examples of people who regularly receive close protection are:

- The British Royal Family
- Foreign Royalty

- The Prime Minister
- A President
- A Head of State
- Certain Ministers in High Office
- Politicians for Certain Events
- Film and TV Celebrities
- Pop Celebrities
- Sports Personalities
- Very Rich People
- Company Executives (CEO / Chairman, etc)
- Families of Protected Persons
- The Pope
- Foreign Diplomats
- An individual who is under a real 'Threat'

No one can truthfully say to a protected person that they are 100% safe at all times! The circumstances surrounding the terrorist attacks in the USA on the 11th September 2001 tragically illustrate this statement. Irrespective of high risks it is extremely unusual for a protected person to completely change their lifestyle to accommodate every security demand placed upon them. Some adjustments will be acceptable and easy to implement, such as improving security around a property or placing their private vehicles in a locked garage. Other areas such as trying to change their daily routine or varying routes to and from work, are a very different kettle of fish. A much more subtle approach is required to encourage a principal to change habits of a lifetime.

In order to reduce risk, extremely robust layers of close protection can be established around a principal. Fortress style security may be implemented around a residence, and much like the White House in Washington DC it can be made extremely difficult for an individual to gain any unauthorised access to someone like the President of the United States of America. If a principal does not move from a well-protected residence, then the risk of anyone achieving some sort of successful attack is minimal. Unfortunately, human nature and a principal's desire to live as normal a life as possible, forces the protected person out into the public domain. It is this situation where their personal risk increases, and it then becomes the role of the Close Protection Group (CPG) to manage the risk.

"JUST A QUIET DINNER TOGETHER — THEY WON'T EVEN KNOW WE WERE OUT"

Threat and Risk

Threat and Risk can be a confusing subject, therefore in this paragraph and in the simplest of terms I will explain the difference. *'Threat'* basically refers to a source of danger to a principal, and once assessed it generally remains the same. *'Risk'* refers to the possibility of danger from a threat, and can vary considerably. As an example, imagine that an extremist group is threatening to attack the Chairman of a Pharmaceutical Company for the company's involvement in animal experimentation. The *threat* is that the group is trying to attack the Chairman, but the *risk* is that they may achieve their aim. Close Protection Operatives can do nothing that will alter the *threat*, as the group will *always* be looking for ways to attack the Chairman. However, as protection personnel we *can* affect the risk by taking appropriate measures to prevent the group from achieving their aim. To summarise, we cannot stop the group from trying *(threat)*, but we can stop them from achieving *(risk)*. It therefore follows that the reality of CP is that you must be ever mindful of the circumstances of an event, the protected person's profile, the wishes of the principal, protocol - and then pro-actively manage the *risk*.

Throughout my years in Royalty Protection I was often asked questions relating to where my team or I as the Team Leader (TL) were strategically positioned around a principal. People would question where protection personnel stood during a drinks reception or the seating arrangements during a meal. This interest stemmed from a desire to be nosey or probed a perceived lack of close protection cover. Each situation was different but my answer was generally the same. Without compromising my security plan, I pointed out that the circumstances of an event, the profile of a principal and their wishes, the protocol requirements and available CP resources determine the appropriate protection response.

This discreet, unobtrusive and flexible approach to CP is a very British style of operation that continually attempts to strike the right balance of security measures. Close protection is not about the use of rigid military style drills, it is about planning and preparing for any eventuality whilst maintaining a flexible response to threats.

A good example of the need for flexibility would be when a protected person unexpectedly decides to do something. An unplanned stop to speak to fans outside a venue, and then sign autographs, can send some close protection teams into an unnecessary panic. If a principal decides to speak to a member of the public, then that is what they will do. CP personnel sometimes have a clouded view about what they are really being employed for. Their role is *not* to dictate a principal's daily schedule or change their programme, but to provide appropriate protection arrangements around anything they choose to do.

From time to time there is a case for close protection personnel to attempt to influence the principal sufficiently to adjust any programme to accommodate security concerns. Very occasionally a CPO will need to be assertive and directly challenge a principal's wishes or decision. My only word of caution with this confrontational approach is that if a team leader wishes to stop a principal from doing something, then he better have a very good reason to support his stance. If the TL cannot objectively support his argument then he may quickly find himself out of a job. This important part of a CPO's role can be quite a complex area to negotiate, and is explored further in the Communication Communication Communication Chapter later in this book.

Threat and Risk Assessment

In the private close protection sector a formal general threat and risk assessment for a principal or event is not normally completed. More often than not they are an expensive commodity to commission, and are full of disclaimers and caveats that reduce their credibility. A far better way of accurately assessing the threat and risk to a principal or venue is to concentrate your intelligence gathering efforts much closer to home.

The best source of information that may indicate a threat or potential problem to a protected person is directly from the principals themselves. This can be raised and established during your initial meeting with a principal, assuming you are fortunate enough to have one. Next are the people who are closely linked to them, such as a member of their family or more often than not, personal staff who have an intimate knowledge of the principal's state of health, work and home environment. Little bits of information can help to build a much bigger picture, such as the persistent fan who will not take 'no' for an answer. They may have written to the principal many times, and been refused requests for meetings or autographs, etc. The next step for them may be to trespass on private property, or pursue a different approach in an attempt to gain access to the principal. Waiting at the entrance to an office or residence is a common strategy used by well wishers or fixated persons. This approach particularly increases the personal risk to a principal when entering or departing from known locations. Unless people outside a venue follow a course of conduct indicating harassment or a fear of violence, waiting in a public place is not an illegal act but it can be very irritating for both a principal and the CP team. Although the vast majority of people who follow this course of action are innocent watchers, there may be the odd individual loitering nearby whose intentions are far more sinister.

A tragic example of this exact scenario was the murder of John Lennon on the 8th December 1980. At just before 11pm John and his wife Yoko were travelling in a limousine when it pulled up at their New York apartment building on Manhattan's Upper West Side. Waiting outside the Dakota building entrance was Mark Chapman, a deranged fixated individual from the Pacific Ocean islands of Hawaii. As John and Yoko walked from their limousine towards the lobby doors of the building, Chapman produced a point 38 calibre revolver from his pocket and fired five shots. John was struck by four of the bullets and despite desperate attempts to save his life he later died of his injuries. During the police investigation it was established that in order to 'seek out' John Lennon, Chapman had travelled thousands of miles from Hawaii to New York. He had made local enquiries and established the exact location of the Lennon apartment in Manhattan. On the morning of the murder he waited outside the Dakota building and even obtained John Lennon's autograph. After that first brief encounter, Chapman must have loitered for many hours waiting for John and Yoko's return to the Dakota building prior to the fatal shooting later that evening.

In the private close protection sector, unfortunately a tight budget and limited resources do not allow CPOs to devote too much time to intelligence gathering or threat and risk assessment. More often than not a CP team will consist of just one CPO assisted by a chauffeur who may or may not be security trained. *With few protection personnel to manage the risk the best approach to effective CP is to be pro-active in your planning, maintain tight control over information about the principal and wherever possible to avoid routine.*

Circumstances of an Event

Provided CP resources are not restrictive, the circumstances of a particular event should always be a major factor in determining the appropriate close protection response. For example, an official visit by a principal to a factory with potentially hostile workers, will have a far greater need for additional CP resources than a private lunch at a country house. A private road journey into the country could be approached far differently to a regular road journey or one through a crime 'hot spot' in a major city. It would be impossible to give you examples of all the different events you are likely to experience. Private events with no advance publicity carry far less risk than a public event where the principal's itinerary is detailed through the media. In 1963 John F Kennedy was probably shot as a direct result of his Dallas motorcade route being widely publicised prior to that fateful day. This allowed Lee Harvey Oswald to plan his assassination meticulously, and ultimately position himself at a high vantage point to fire those fatal shots. So, as a general guide, if no advance publicity has been given to an event and no members of the public or media are aware of the principal's itinerary, it follows that the resultant security risk must be a lower one. The simple graph below illustrates how risk can vary many times throughout a day.

Variations of Risk

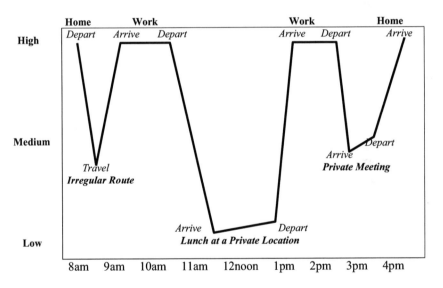

You will particularly note from this graph that persons departing from and arriving at home, work or other known or predictable locations are potentially very high-risk times for a VIP. History has repeatedly shown by the many serious or fatal attacks detailed earlier in the book, that these times are when most incidents occur. Arriving and departing at known locations should be when a CP team is at their highest state of alertness.

Profile

Although in the last section I emphasised the importance of the circumstances of an event, the profile of a principal is equally important in determining the appropriate close protection response. In many ways the two are closely linked, but a principal with a high profile can often require far more resources than a principal with a high threat. The examples following will assist in explaining the difference.

Imagine that you have been employed to provide close protection to the Chief Executive Officer (CEO) of an American Company who has been assessed at a high threat. This may be due to unpopular management decisions relating to employee redundancies or the nature of his business. It would be in his best interest to go about his daily duties unnoticed, and attempt to maintain as low a profile as possible. The possibility of the CEO being recognised by members of the public is unlikely, therefore when he undertakes irregular private journeys and activities the risk is minimal.

Conversely, imagine that you have been employed to provide close protection for an extremely well known film actor who is instantly recognisable worldwide. Generally the threat to this type of person would be low, but their high profile status would demand a completely different type of close protection response. Attendance at a film premiere will merit much media attention, and undoubtedly attract large numbers of the general public requiring some sort of crowd control. In fact every time a well-known film actor ventures out into the public arena, even privately, they are highly likely to be recognised and attract some sort of public interest.

With these examples in mind the profile of an individual can therefore be determined by how well known they are, and how much public and media attention that person generates. An additional factor to consider when assessing the appropriate level of close protection cover, is the fact that some celebrities actively seek to increase their public profile at every opportunity. Many of them are 'orchestrated' by their Public Relations Manager or on an ego trip eager to seek publicity whenever possible. It may be undertaking an informal walkabout outside a world film premiere, or a publicity stunt guaranteed to maximise media coverage. A well-known celebrity who is a low threat can still be at risk from the more intrusive media who have potential for much conflict with the principal and can cause the most trouble. As they say in the celebrity world, there is no such thing as bad publicity!

Personal Profile

An area often skimmed or overlooked by CPO's is the personal profile of the principal. Main threats such as terrorism, criminality, stalkers, kidnapping and the potential threat from extremist groups is normally well assessed and appropriately managed. What is not so obvious and accurately analysed, is the personal profile of the protected person. Nationality, politics, corporate position, religion or cultural background is generally identified, but the VIP's health and lifestyle is often overlooked.

A large percentage of protected persons are middle aged, overworked, overweight, relatively unfit and lead a hectic 24/7 lifestyle. In addition to the statistical health problems for the over 50s (ulcers, diabetes, angina, high blood pressure, bad circulation, etc), they generally suffer from a pressured work environment where food is often snatched between meetings. This hectic work schedule regularly leads to a lack of rest or sleep, with a resultant tiredness where the principal can suffer from exhaustion. If your VIP closely matches any of the circumstances outlined above, I strongly recommend you undertake an in-depth personal profile of their health. It is good practice to carry your personal medical kit at all times, and as a back-up to the worst case scenario be in possession of additional prescription medicine for your principal.

The Wishes of the Principal

The wishes of the principal is one of the most important areas of close protection to grasp, as ultimately the protected person will always maintain a level of control over any security arrangements. A fundamental principle of professional CP is to avoid routine and regular road journeys, however for a protected person it can be one of the most difficult things to accept. The wishes of the principal can often hinder any close protection arrangements by raising the risk, and history has shown that those wishes regularly do.

The most tragic example of this would be Dallas, USA in 1963 when John F Kennedy's insistence on not having security specifically around his vehicle, directly contributed to his assassination. It may be that the presence of US Secret Service Agents around the vehicle would not have prevented the assassination attempt, but it would certainly have made it much more difficult to achieve.

One of the key roles of a professional team leader is to quickly identify their principal's likes and dislikes, particularly in respect of the provision of close protection. In establishing these preferences and a good working relationship with the principal, it is more likely that situations where there is potential for a conflict of interests can be avoided. Most protected persons have quite strong views about the provision of CP, but will generally accept the security arrangements provided they are appropriate to the circumstances. In a public environment a CP team can and should be more noticeable, but whenever possible you must take the opportunity to blend into the background and give the principal space. These situations occur much more frequently in a private scenario, and should be seized at every opportunity. By not being seen in these situations the CP team will send a clear signal of their understanding of the needs and wishes of the principal. The principal is unlikely to verbally acknowledge this discretion, but you can be assured that they will have mentally noted it.

Protocol

Protocol is basically a combination of rules, formalities, traditions, customs and etiquette pertaining to a particular event. A quick example of protocol in the United Kingdom is how on meeting someone for the first time, people tend to offer a verbal greeting combined with the shaking of hands. This British custom is typical of many things that occur during an event and can best be described as programme protocols.

More often than not security arrangements come a poor second to the needs of protocol, and regularly clash with best practice of close protection. It is extremely difficult to change a programme purely on the grounds of security. In my 'Golden Rules of Close Protection' (Chapter 8), if you wish to adjust any planned arrangements then be adequately prepared to justify your decisions. My strong advice is that if you don't have a good reason to change protocol as part of a planned programme, then plan your close protection arrangements accordingly and say nothing. Keep your powder dry for a battle worth fighting!

Close Protection Resources (Public v Private)

For events protected by personnel from either the police or any of the three armed services, more often than not generous resources are allocated to a close protection task. As an example, if you take the wedding of His Royal Highness The Prince of Wales and Camilla Parker-Bowles on the 9th April 2005 at Windsor Castle, the media made much comment about the extent of the security measures and the resultant cost to the public purse. Although it is important and healthy for any public expenditure to be questioned and scrutinised, it should be born in mind that for this particular wedding two Chief Police Officers had certain responsibilities. Firstly, the Commissioner of Police for the Metropolis (London) is responsible for the personal protection of all members of the British Royal Family, and unusually for the Metropolitan Police Service (MPS) within the grounds of Windsor Castle, which is outside the Metropolitan Police District (MPD). Secondly, the Chief Constable of the Thames Valley Police had responsibilities for any security measures outside the grounds of Windsor Castle, and in particular protecting the many thousands of members of the public who visited Windsor Town Centre on that day.

If the police presence had been inadequate and an incident or improvised explosive device had detonated, apart from the horror of such an event you can just imagine the venomous media criticism that would have followed. It is such a serious issue that a Chief Police Officer could potentially loose his or her job, as a direct result of an incident due to a perceived lack of security. This typical example illustrates the tough decisions that have to be made by police with national responsibilities, and the constant pressure always to get the appropriate policing arrangements right.

Provision of close protection within the private security industry, however, requires a very different approach. With no national responsibilities and only the principal to protect, the key factor in deciding the level of close protection cover simply comes down to cost. The two main issues are: i) How much is someone prepared to pay for personal protection? and ii) How much protective cover does the principal actually want?

Assuming that cost is not an issue, there are many permutations of close protection cover that can be provided, and some organisations favour a 'numbers' approach. Unless the threat and risk assessment merits a very large close protection team, my own view is a small team is both discreet and generally more efficient. As team leader I would choose to have a qualified CPO to drive the VIP car, and preferably someone who is also a specially trained security driver. This often-underrated role is integral to an effective close protection team, particularly considering that when mobile with a principal the driver controls virtually everything you do. Without being too dramatic, a poor decision on their part can sometimes mean the difference between life and death.

To support me I would employ four other CPOs, one of whom would act as the driver of a back-up close protection vehicle. These additional resources provide great versatility to the CPG. They can be split to provide a two-person Security Advance Party (SAP) to go ahead and 'secure' any venue prior to the arrival of the principal. The two remaining CPOs are then still available to provide mobile back-up protection as required.

In reality, the likelihood of a principal being willing and able to pay for six CPOs on a private close protection assignment is slim. You often end up with just a team leader plus a driver for the principal's vehicle. In these circumstances many close protection compromises have to be made, requiring the CP team to prioritise tasks, undoubtedly reducing the effectiveness of the protective cover. At the end of the day you are paid by the principal to manage the risk with the resources you are allocated. If you are not happy with the situation and don't like the heat, then you will just have to get out of the kitchen!

3 PROFESSIONAL STANDARDS

I place a huge amount of emphasis and importance on an individual's communication skills. Although they should always come at the top of any list of competencies, I thought long and hard about placing 'Professional Standards' ahead of the Communication Communication Communication Chapter in this book. My rationale is a simple one, and that is there are aspects of professional standards that can influence people and particularly a principal, long before they have the opportunity to assess and value your interpersonal communication skills. Therefore it is this very important area of personal image projection and the early opportunities to impress people, that I am going to concentrate on first.

I accept that in this modern day and age I shouldn't 'tell' people how to dress or present themselves in any given situation. However, the reality is that in a protection context where you are in close proximity of a principal and everyone around them, high professional standards really matter. In many respects the Close Protection Operative (CPO) represents the principal in everything they do. Whether it is planning an event, organising a visit or just accompanying them, your closeness transmits a message of association! Unusual individual fashion styles, poor personal hygiene and a scruffy appearance will not please principals or secure your place at their side.

Be under no misunderstanding that first impressions count for a lot. It is a fact that despite whether it is politically correct or not, people will form an opinion within the first few seconds of setting eyes on you. This visual assessment may not provide a full picture of your skills, but can often be the swaying factor in a decision to employ you. Putting it bluntly, you could be the most highly trained close protection operative in the world, but if you were unshaven, wore a food-stained tie and had bad breath you probably wouldn't get the job.

Principals demand high professional standards because they are used to them, they are less tolerant than others, they are paying the wages and they do not like to be embarrassed. Professional standards covers a wide range of issues, and in a close protection context I will address them in a logical order. Ignore them at your peril!

Dress and Appearance

In the private sector the vast majority of principals are wealthy, middle-aged executives whose clothing will be both expensive and generally of a conservative nature. A CPO must blend into the protected person's world, and therefore your choice of clothing should always be dictated by the principal's chosen attire. Always take the dress code lead from the principal, but my strong advice would be *not* to out-dress them. Wearing similar good quality clothing would be eminently suitable, but I would also advise against wearing expensive designer clothes. This approach could be viewed as up-staging the principal's status and subtly challenging their position as the VIP.

As a guide, at a first meeting or formal interview the best form of dress for men is a clean, well-pressed dark blue or dark grey suit. Some CP operatives favour wearing a black suit, however my view is that matched with a black shirt and tie there is a risk of giving the impression that you are either a sombre person or doubling as a funeral assistant. For women, similar suits, conservatively patterned dresses, skirts, blouses and jackets would be equally acceptable, but they must also be functional and relatively loose fitting to allow you to undertake the close protection role.

Trouser belts should be black and generally match the colour of your shoes. Most formal suits should be complemented with a long-sleeve shirt, preferably white, and a classy touch can be added by wearing a smart pair of cufflinks. Alternative shirts should be plain in colour, pastel or very slightly patterned. Loud stripes and check patterns stand out too much, and can be interpreted as a fashion statement. Purchase ties of a high quality, silk being ideal, and always choose conservative styles. Abstract patterns, repetitive names, embedded photographs or ties implying commercial advertising must be avoided. Remember you are with the principal all the time, therefore your choice of clothing transmits a message that can directly reflect their image.

CPO's spend long periods of time standing and therefore investment in quality footwear will be money well spent. Footwear needs to be of a plain style and ideally in black leather or similar finish. Loudly coloured shoes, trainers, heavy boots, particularly industrial or cowboy style, must be avoided at all costs. A pair of comfortable, sturdy, plain or brogue-style black shoes, have the advantage of being functional, effective as a defensive aid if necessary and look extremely smart in an executive environment. Ladies should choose to wear similar quality flatter shoes and particularly avoid high heels. They are detrimental to your balance and speed of movement that is critical in the CP environment. Socks should be plain or only slightly patterned, and closely match the colour of your suit. Brightly coloured socks or those sporting large writing or pictures such as cartoon characters or your favourite Premiership football club are definitely out!

Smart business clothing described above is entirely appropriate for the majority of executive CP assignments. However, if your principal is a child or well-known rock singer, a different approach to your CP dress code is required. In these circumstances it is unlikely that a formal suit would be the right choice of clothing. The correct approach would be to wear more casual attire appropriate to achieve your protection objectives whilst still maintaining the grey man or woman image. When in doubt, take the lead from the principal.

The issue of hairstyle is guaranteed to generate much discussion, particularly with women, therefore my views should be seen as 'guidance' strictly based on my own observation. The wearing of long hair can be a silly distraction to your core role in CP, as it often requires much grooming and regularly necessitates sweeping it away from your eyes. Brightly coloured hair streaks or shaved designs on the head should not be entertained in any circumstances. They stand out as a fashion statement and more importantly draw attention to yourself in a role where you want to avoid it. A relatively short hairstyle is ideal, but the addition of excessive hair gel or cream is not complimentary or appropriate for a CPO. Shaved heads can occasionally be acceptable, but in general they give the impression of an aggressive type of person like a 'bouncer' which principals are unlikely to favour. If you are normally clean-shaven, which I recommend, you must ensure that your last shave was a recent one with no 12-hour shadows.

The wearing of sunglasses often generates mixed views amongst experienced close protection personnel, with some saying that you should never wear them. Others, including myself, take the view that they have an important place in CP, particularly in extremely sunny weather conditions. I can remember many occasions, particularly on Caribbean islands, when the sun was so bright that the wearing of sunglasses was the only way to effectively observe activity around the principal without squinting. The best advice I can offer is that sunglasses should be considered yet another specialist tool in the CP kit bag, and they should not be worn constantly as a fashion accessory to project a steely image.

It has been known for a principal to ask for a CPO to be removed from a team, solely because they didn't particularly like something about their

Meeting the principal for the first time!

clothing or general appearance. It could be brown shoes with a grey suit or yellow socks for an evening function. It matters not, but close protection can be a cruel environment. You can see that the clear message for a CPO's dress and appearance is conservative with a big 'C'.

Punctuality and Reliability

One of my golden rules of close protection is: *'Always be Punctual (NB At least 15 Minutes early)'*. The importance of this point cannot be overstated, particularly as the principal is likely to be paying for you to be available 24 hours a day. They do not expect *you* to keep *them* waiting, and although you are not a servant in the strict sense of the word, principals will demand that

Sorry I'm late I didn't hear the alarm clock!

you be ready to leave before them. A plausible reason or excuse for your lateness on the first occasion may be reluctantly accepted, however a principal is unlikely to be so sympathetic a second or third time.

Accurate timekeeping and punctuality is the bedrock of good close protection, and can enhance that special principal/close protection operative relationship. It demonstrates that you are extremely reliable, and sends the right messages of your motivation, enthusiasm and conscientiousness.

Personal Hygiene

The importance of personal hygiene cannot be overstated. Think about your own standards and experiences of other people's personal hygiene and ask the following question: "Which poor standards of personal hygiene annoy you the most?" I guarantee that you will be thinking of one or more of the following points:

Body Odour

Body Odour and the great unwashed is a guaranteed way of only being in a CP role for a very short period of time. Whilst employed as a Personal Protection Officer, it was common for me to have at least two baths or showers a day! A full-time CPO is rarely required to be on duty for less than a 14-hour shift. In this time you may well be with a principal undertaking activities such as walking, shopping, travelling, business meetings, sporting events, and so on. Apart from a natural geographical environment that may well be humid or dusty, an individual will sweat quite normally and need to freshen up every so often. You cannot hide body odour from people who are in close proximity to you, particularly when travelling together in a motor vehicle. Without teaching people to suck eggs, and there are no rigid rules on this, my strong recommendation would be to suggest a bath or shower first thing in the morning which is repeated before going out for an evening event.

Body Sprays / Perfume and After Shave

The opposite to body odour is the excessive use of the wide variety of body sprays, deodorants, perfume and after-shave. These products often make wild claims of 24-hour odour protection via spicy fragrances or scent that keeps you feeling fresh, confident and ready for anything (whatever that means). Each container or bottle is often accompanied by warnings that solvent abuse can instantly kill, the fragrance should only be applied in a well-ventilated area and wherever possible to avoid inhalation. If the application of these sprays is intended to project an inviting smell for you and others, I am not sure how anyone can avoid some sort of inhalation!

Excessive use of body deodorants and perfume can be over-powering, quite revolting, and in my experience encourage me to want to get away from someone. I do not suggest that a ban on using sprays and potions is the 'Directing Staff' answer to CP, but a very conservative application is undoubtedly the best approach. One thing for sure is that using too much spray, perfume or after-shave, is a guaranteed solution for mosquito bites but will also kill off your professional working relationship with the principal.

Bad Breath and Chewing Gum

Both bad breath and chewing gum can be devastating to a CPO's image, as you rely heavily on communicating with a wide range of people to effectively carry out your role. Very often someone with bad breath cannot detect it themselves, as they are with the odour all the time and it has become natural to them. A habit that can be a particularly unpleasant experience is to talk and observe someone who is constantly chewing gum. Apart from it being an irritating habit for the observer, there is nothing worse than seeing and hearing someone constantly opening and closing their mouth. You can unwittingly be welcoming a view of your recent dental treatments, and breathing the smell of the gum through every word and gesture. You can just imagine what it must be like to be on the receiving end of gold fillings and the aroma from 'strawberry-flavoured' gum.

Although CPO's undertake a role that is more detached from the principal, it is vitally important that they also demonstrate the highest of professional standards. Principals regularly speak to all members of the protection team, and even occasionally travel in a support protection vehicle. Remember that you indirectly represent the principal in everything you do, particularly when communicating with others to make some security arrangements. Bad breath, poor personal hygiene and your general demeanour will be noticed, and could be brought to the attention of the principal. It is not uncommon for people to mention to the principal various activities or behaviour of the Close Protection Group (CPG). It could be a desire to praise you, criticise you or just to tell a story about the security arrangements. There is also the jealousy factor about people close to a protected person. Someone may well take great delight in mentioning your strong garlic breath just to dent your impeccable image or slur your previous good name.

Hands, Fingers and Nails

The state of your hands is an area often ignored or overlooked by many people, particularly men. Apart from stating the obvious about ensuring your hands are clean at all times, you should be mindful of the way your hands look and feel. For example, if you are a keen gardener or motor mechanic, a hardened, scratched or oil stained look on your hands will not be welcome. Oil and earth-engrained skin and nails can take several washes to completely eradicate. Well-clipped and groomed nails that are not chewed or bitten, is a pre-requisite for the CPO role. I know that some men will laugh at this advice, but I would strongly advocate the use of a good hand/nail brush, followed by the application of a hand moisturiser. Remember shaking hands is often the first or second contact you make with a principal, their family, staff, team colleagues or other security partners. Hands and nails are a visual indicator of your general hygiene standards and it is very important to give the right impression.

Swearing

I am sad to have to report that in the 21st century swearing has become a more acceptable part of everyday language. It seems to me that the continual use of swear words is far more a youth habit, where many people curse without thinking of the words they are actually using and are often immune to any offence it may cause to others nearby. This complete disregard for other people's feelings, particularly children and the elderly, demonstrates a ruthless selfishness and lack of personal values. Anyone reading this Chapter whose own vocabulary is regularly littered with expletives would be well advised to change their habits quickly. When swearing has become a cultural thing where the user is unaware of what he is saying, it is unlikely that he will not swear in the presence of a protected person. You may think that using the *f* word or other foul language is totally acceptable in modern day vocabulary, but I can guarantee that a principal will be unamused and not support that view.

The Unmentionables

Before putting this section in the 'Professional Standards' Chapter of the book, I hesitated and reflected on whether I was insulting you, the reader's intelligence. On consulting with colleagues and reflecting on some of my own experiences, I decided that however unpalatable, the message might be the subject needs airing.

Smelly feet are the natural but unpleasant result of excessive sweating inside your shoes, and my strong advice is to change your socks and shoes twice a day. Examples of unnecessary crude activities are burping, breaking-wind, spitting or picking your nose and they are all totally unacceptable. If you need to blow your nose, then please use a handkerchief and make sure it is a clean one! Get into the habit of changing your handkerchief every day.

A clean handkerchief was the very thing that helped enhance my professional working relationship with a female member of the Royal Family. I was on duty as the Personal Protection Officer on a helicopter trip to an event outside of London. The rural nature of the visit necessitated landing in a field followed by a short car journey to the venue. On walking from the helicopter to the VIP car, the principal trod in some animal faeces. With only a short car journey to complete, there was little time to hide the embarrassment. I gave instructions to slow the vehicle convoy down, without informing the accompanying entourage of the exact reasons why. I came to the principal's rescue with the offer and subsequent use of my clean handkerchief to clean the dirty shoe. I swore the VIP car driver to secrecy, and after a discreet disposal of my soiled handkerchief, no one on the royal visit was any the wiser. This incident undoubtedly enhanced my position with the principal.

Smoking

My advice to smokers is simple – *Give Up!* Your body and clothes smell due to the absorption of smoke. Your hands, fingers and teeth can show nicotine stains and it is bad for your health. Smoking is rapidly becoming socially unacceptable throughout the world, is often banned in public places, and is an unnecessary distraction from your core role of close protection. It is made worse by the fact that generally principals do not like it. Need I say any more?

Diplomacy

A very important but often overlooked area of the professional standards required of a CPO, is the need to be extremely sensitive to situations and the needs and feelings of others. It may be a domestic problem that is developing around a principal, or a CPO colleague who has a particular welfare issue at home. Whatever the situation, a sensitive caring approach is needed, and that may require you to just give someone some space, or offer them an ear to share their problem. Properly reading a scenario can be difficult, but many indicators will point you to a particular problem. A principal's body language or the odd isolated comment can add to a 'jigsaw puzzle' of clues pointing to a particular issue. A CPO must be hypersensitive to these signs as principals rarely share their problems with you or explain how they are feeling. Above all, being constantly approachable and supportive without taking sides, will often provide you with the perfect solution to the situation. A balanced approach to sensitive issues allows you to maintain a professional relationship with the principal without getting personally involved.

Temperament

Closely linked to the previous section is temperament, which is a key competency necessary to be a professional and effective CPO. If you are employed as the person responsible for establishing a safe environment in which a principal can live and work, it follows that you must be a confident individual who demonstrates a calm nature at all times. An even-tempered CPO, who displays an ability to remain unflustered in any given situation, promotes a principal confidence much more than words can ever achieve. Panic is infectious, and if a CPO displays this characteristic it is guaranteed to spiral the principal to the same state. I have always been of the view that people should do less talking-up a good job, and concentrate more on letting their performance do the talking. A cool, calm temperament will develop your own confidence, and can be such a strong indicator of your overall personality and character.

Honesty

In regulating close protection, the employment of CPO's with a hidden history of serious criminal convictions will become a thing of the past. This very welcome change will dramatically reduce the risk of criminal types exploiting their wealthy principals. Apart from the obvious close proximity that a CPO enjoys with a protected person, for criminal types the opportunities to steal from or defraud them are immense. Fraudulent expense claims or theft of cash from a gratuities float, could be concealed without much difficulty. To build up a principal's trust for you and develop an excellent working relationship, I propose that you should go out of your way to make a 'statement' about your honesty. A good example would be that whenever you legitimately spend the principal's money, ensure you get some sort of receipt in support of your claim. It may only be a scribbled note for a taxi fare, but the very presence of a receipt makes a silent reference about how much you can be trusted. This overt act displays your high standards of honesty and integrity, and will be another building block in developing the trust and chemistry so important in the principal / CPO relationship.

Mobile Phones

In this modern era, mobile phones are now an every day part of most peoples' lives, and are viewed as an essential personal item. The communication advantages to personnel employed as CPO's are obvious, but there are some distinct disadvantages that are not so obvious.

Protected persons by nature tend to closely guard their private lives, therefore the use of a mobile phone camera, video and particularly voice-recorders around a principal or their family should be strictly avoided. Even the use of a camera to record some sort of innocent scenic picture can be interpreted in the wrong way, and potentially may damage any trust a principal has in you.

I am sure that everyone has experienced a mobile phone call received at an inconvenient moment. If the call is a particularly important one, then most people will go out of their way to engage in conversation with the caller necessary to conclude it. When working with a principal the use of mobile phones must be kept to a minimum. It can be very irritating for a protected person to be accompanied by someone who is constantly talking on his phone. I work on the principle of 'no news is good news'. If things are going according to plan, then do not feel a burning desire to communicate just for the sake of it. Get into the habit of setting your mobile phone to a discreet mode, in order to receive calls or text messages without a loud ringtone or it being obvious to the principal. Do not engage in private conversations when in close proximity to the protected person, and if your mobile phone is provided for business use only then avoid private calls at all costs. If you receive and identify a private call at an inconvenient time then just ignore it. They can leave a message on your recorded voice mail and you can ring them back later. In CP it is not always 'good to talk'.

Continuing Professional Development

Historically Continuing Professional Development (CPD) training in the UK commercial CP sector, is a rare and relatively unpracticed activity. The limited continuation training that is available, has focused on activity-based refresher courses such as evasive driving, firearms training for hostile environments and some tactical CP modules. What is even more concerning is the fact that a large percentage of UK based CPO's working today (2006), have never undertaken any formal CP training whatsoever. They have been selected solely as a direct result of serving in a particular military regiment or police force, and given a helping hand into a CP job through the old-boys network. I understand the importance of employee recommendation but employers who solely favour this prejudiced system of selection, regularly overlook many suitably skilled and well-trained CPO's from a purely civilian background.

The situation I describe above is most unsatisfactory and I am delighted to report is gradually changing. As a direct result of the Private Security Industry Act 2001 and the birth of the Security Industry Authority (SIA), regulation for CP will eventually clean up the sector. Licensing for people working in

Close Protection came into effect across England and Wales at the same time. On 20 March 2006 it became illegal to work in Close Protection without an SIA CP licence (this applies to contract staff only). It will also be an offence for a company to employ any contract staff in the role of a CPO in England and Wales who do not hold an SIA CP Licence. With SIA regulation and the on-going drive to raise professional standards and encourage higher education CPD through the Protective Security Management Foundation Degree Course at Buckinghamshire Chilterns University College, the future for properly trained professional CPOs looks very much brighter.

4 COMMUNICATION COMMUNICATION COMMUNICATION

Chapter 1 of this book probed the merits and limitations of what I describe as the close protection hard skills. It also attempted to put them into context compared to the reality of the CP role. I view communication as the number one softer skill integral to being a really professional and successful CPO. In this Chapter I explore the many different areas of interpersonal communication, and the following analogy illustrates support for my argument favouring a stronger emphasis on the softer skills of CP compared to the equally important area of police firearms training. I served in the Metropolitan Police Service (MPS) for just over thirty years, and was an Authorised Firearms Officer (AFO) from 1974 until I retired in 2001. During those twenty-seven years I received extensive initial and advanced firearms training on the following weapons: Webley revolver, Smith and Wesson revolver models 10, 36 and 64, the Browning self-loading pistol (Mark 1 and 2) and finally the Glock self-loading pistol. I must have fired tens of thousands of rounds of ammunition in an attempt to perfect my drawing and shooting skills. I am delighted to say that throughout my service I never had an occasion that merited the necessity to either draw or use a firearm as a means of defence. However, throughout this same period and particularly when employed on close protection duties I had occasion to professionally speak to thousands of people. These statistics are not in any way designed to criticise the necessity of police firearms training, but more to highlight how important communication is both as a generic skill and more specifically within a CP environment.

What Is Communication?

Do I really need to cover this subject? Surely, we are all well aware of exactly what communication is. Isn't it just socialising and talking to other people on a daily basis? If communication was just that simple you could skip this Chapter. However, it is far more complex than that and is often the key to CP!

Any contact with other people is a form of communication. Whether it is a letter, an e-mail, a glance, a stare, a smile, a nod, a grin or a touch, all these actions and gestures transmit varying messages. These messages can make or break any initial contact or relationship whether it is professional or personal. Think of your own experience of work-related or personal relationships that have broken down, and I guarantee that communication, or a lack of it has played a major part in the outcome. Impressing someone from that first introduction and then through a protracted period of working together, has more to do with interpersonal communication than any specific practical skills. It is only once you have built a good working relationship over a period of time, that you can be much more assertive and challenging with a principal. In my experience, protected persons value their CPO's honest, professional advice and opinions far more than a sycophantic person who gives a 'yes sir' answer to everything. Occasionally a situation can develop when you need to advise a principal on a particular course of action that will be unpopular. Assuming your suggestion is ultimately the right option, the principal may not immediately thank you or shower you with praise. However, they often reflect and appreciate your sound judgement and honest professional advice without necessarily showing it. I often used to say that having given unpopular advice to a principal, their later silence was a good indicator that they ultimately agreed with your recommended course of action. As a general observation VIP's are not very good at admitting they are wrong or apologising, particularly to members of their own staff for whom they are paying the wages.

I have now set the scene detailing some of the opportunities to utilise your interpersonal skills with the principal. I do not profess to be a communications expert, but with a thirty-year police career behind me, I am well placed to make comment on this competency area.

Writing Skills

In close protection a CPO's ability to communicate in the written form is often considered of secondary importance compared to the operational role. Networking aside, this is a mistake, as you would normally have to take part in a written application process to secure a CP contract. This is often the first contact with a potential client or principal, and if so it will always precede any opportunity to demonstrate your skills as an effective operator. In most work environments an example of your written presentational skills are often the first thing that people judge you on. It may be a letter accompanying a Curriculum Vitae (CV), or an e-mail making an enquiry about a job vacancy. Whichever written method you select to make initial contact, my strong advice is to take your time over it and get it right at the first attempt. In this modern day and age there are relatively few acceptable excuses for getting this part of the communication process wrong. You can draft your correspondence as many times as you like, and you have the opportunity to seek the guidance of friends and possibly professionals. Public libraries have excellent research facilities and staff will always help you in some way or another. The advance of computer word processor software with spelling, grammar and thesaurus technical support makes preparing a letter or CV a relatively simple process. Remember that a first letter with an accompanying CV, is often your only opportunity to impress someone enough to invite you to attend an interview. It was my written application to join Royalty Protection in 1979 that started the process resulting in a 22-year specialist CP career within the MPS.

As the vast majority of CPO's or security consultants are self-employed there is also a need for your pre and post CP contract paperwork to be of a high standard. For consultants a thoroughly prepared professional report detailing matters such as risk analysis and recommendations are essential to the role. Invoices or expenses submitted with errors in spelling, grammar or mathematics would send the wrong message to a principal or client about your honesty, intelligence and lack of attention to detail. Coaching may be necessary to improve this area of your communication skills, but be assured it will be time well spent and very worthwhile.

Non-Verbal Communication

Without necessarily being conscious of it, people are constantly sending out signals to others by the use of their overt or passive non-verbal communication. It may be a smile or a wave but everything you do transmits various signs about your mood, attitude, demeanour, interest or disinterest in someone or something. Think of an occasion when you were speaking with a colleague and they constantly looked away or were easily distracted. I guarantee this irritated you as it gave the impression that they were not interested in what you were saying.

Some examples of people who are particularly good at transmitting and interpreting non-verbal communication signals are politicians, journalists and news presenters. It is common to see them on television listening attentively whilst maintaining direct eye contact with others and nodding profusely. This overt style reflects their professional role of projecting themselves through the television medium and getting a message across to millions of viewers.

If you are addressing a group of 50 people and the presentation is being televised live to millions of people around the UK, it would be foolish to ignore your non-verbal communication, particularly to the wider audience. The media accompanying members of the British Royal family at public functions would often scrutinise non-verbal communication (NVC) signals between a principal and people around them. Fortunately most of the signals were positive, but occasionally there were areas of polite disagreement that the press took great delight in reporting. One of the best examples of this was a much-used photograph of TRH The Prince and Princess of Wales in the back of a car looking in opposite directions. This pose was just before the announcement of their marriage separation, and inferred their body language said it all. This type of story was the 'bread and butter' of tabloid reporters or freelance writers whose sole intention was to write about something other than opening buildings or serious speeches.

Listening Ability

Effective listening is an extremely important communication skill, but rarely receives the prominence that it actually merits. It is very common for people to spend more time talking than listening, whereas a person should really spend about 60% of their time listening. Just actively listening to principals and others in a close protection environment will always provide you with useful information to assist in your day-to-day CP assignments. I do not suggest that you overtly listen to private conversations, but sometimes you cannot help but overhear a conversation about some future arrangements. It may be a departure time or plans to go out one evening, but the most important thing is that you are now aware of something that will affect you and your CP team. You must master the mental ability to absorb what is being said around you, as you have to get it right first time and won't have an opportunity for clarification!

A very important competency required of a CP Team Leader is the ability to make good decisions for the benefit of the team as a whole. Before making any long-term policy decisions I would always advocate seeking and listening to any suggestions from your team members. They will respect the fact that you listened to their views and provided them with an opportunity to comment on a particular issue. Ultimately you may make a decision that the team disagree with, but at least they will have had an opportunity to express their thoughts and opinions.

Silence

CPOs and particularly Team Leaders are by nature confident individuals who like to engage in general conversation with principals, team members and staff. Protected persons generally view CPOs as just other members of staff, and they do not feel under any obligation to talk to them unless they particularly choose to do so. This atmosphere of silence with the principal can be an uneasy area for Team Leaders and other CPOs to manage. The absence of discussion can often give the impression that you are being ignored or frozen out, but in my experience it is often just the circumstances of a particular time that dictated a quieter period. It may be that the principal has just had a disagreement with someone, and invariably the last thing he then wants to do is make general conversation with a member of the CP team. They could also be deep in thought about an important business meeting, a forthcoming presentation or writing a major speech to shareholders. Silence could be for any number of reasons but whatever the situation do not get unnecessarily concerned about it, just continue to professionally undertake your role. When times are quiet never feel that you have a duty to engage the principal in conversation. The next time you meet it is highly likely that you will be unable to stop them from talking, so value the quiet times! Silence should be considered golden and greatly contributes to the bubble of serenity that is the very essence of good close protection around your principal.

Communication With The Principal

Chapter 5 of this book specifically deals with the professional working relationship with the principal. There are quite naturally some skill areas that overlap different Chapters of the book, so here I will focus on the mechanics of communication rather than the chemistry of a professional working relationship.

The CP team leader has the closest proximity to a principal and all the activities that he or she undertakes. This position places you at the heart of everything the protected person does, from work-related issues to the intimacy of their private lives. There are very few issues that a team leader does not eventually become aware of and, therefore, a very discreet and sensitive approach is always required. Circumstances can dictate that a team leader may have to delegate certain tasks to other members of his team. Therefore they will also become aware of sensitive issues pertaining to the principal, so they too have to be mindful of their position of trust. This intimate principal knowledge makes it all the more important for members of the CPG to demonstrate the utmost discretion. Even the most innocent disclosure of private information about a principal or their family can lead to a CPO's removal from a team.

In the early days of establishing your professional working relationship with a principal, follow three of my golden rules namely: i) 'Generally, speak when spoken to', ii) 'Don't make idle and silly conversation', and iii) 'Try to avoid politics and religion'. I am not suggesting that you should constantly remain silent in the presence of a principal, but let them take the initiative in conversation and view this time as a settling in period. When the protected person does engage you in conversation, it will normally be either to establish some facts or just to be polite. For example it may be to enquire how long a road journey will take, or to ask if you are married and have children. Your answers must be honest, brief and accurate. Any hint of lying or giving a misleading answer will be interpreted as evidence that you are untrustworthy. Once you are labelled with this type of reputation, it is virtually impossible to shake it off. My strong advice at all times is: 'Don't lie, be honest and don't waffle'. If you do not know the answer to a question then say you don't know, but make sure you follow it up with a comment like: "But I will find out Sir and get back to you later". This response signals to the principal that you are a person who is both honest and thorough. By stating that you will establish the answer to the question later, allows you to 'park' the issue for now and address it when you feel it is appropriate. If the matter is urgent then as the team leader you could delegate the enquiry to a colleague, allowing you to continue to focus on your core role with the principal. The principal will remember your promise to obtain an answer, so make sure you return to the issue later, bringing it to a satisfactory conclusion. This approach will continue to develop your relationship and rapport with the protected person, whilst subtly reinforcing your honesty and reliability.

General Knowledge

I remember at school that teachers would constantly labour the importance of reading a wide range of written material to improve my English, grammar and general knowledge. Books, fiction or non-fiction, magazines and quality newspapers, particularly broadsheets, were favoured as recommended reading material. I paid scant regard to this sound advice at the time and it was only much later in life that I realised the significance of it. It is a tremendous advantage to be well read and able to participate in a discussion on a subject matter outside your specialist area of security. Not only will it dispel the view that security personnel are of a lower intelligence, but it will also help develop your relationship with the VIP, their family, staff and your CP team. As a CPO and particularly a TL you can spend a lot of time with your principal, so being able to converse with them on a wide range of subjects is a distinct advantage.

Although I am a strong advocate of broadening a CPO's general knowledge, I am also realistic that a person cannot have an in-depth view of every subject. A few years ago, I undertook an assignment with a VIP visitor from Japan, whose specialist area of research was Nanotechnology and its application for a broad range of industries. Most of the University meetings I attended were at Professor level, and the discussions were of a highly technical nature. Travelling with the VIP between the various appointments, I was eventually asked my specific views on nanotechnology. I immediately stated that it was not a subject I knew anything about, but acknowledged that as a result of the VIP meetings I would be a lot wiser. If you have no understanding of a particular subject matter, then don't lie, be honest and just admit it. Better to be marginally embarrassed over your lack of knowledge, than waffle or lie and potentially lose both the principal's trust and employment!

Humour

The appropriate use of humour can be an effective tool in the protection operative's kit bag. I do not advocate that every time you see the principal you should be cracking jokes or acting the clown, but when the circumstances are right a funny comment can be a powerful communication tool. I often refer to the fact that you can say virtually anything you like, provided you have a smile on your face. That smile will transmit a non-verbal message that generally connects with the principal, and will inevitably strengthen the relationship. If you can tune-in to what makes a protected person laugh, then it can emphasise a CPO's more human nature and make you a more likeable person (extremely important in any relationship whether personal or professional).

On the other side of the coin, the use of inappropriate humour or crude jokes can be destructive to the relationship between a principal and his CPO. Avoid this approach at all costs, and even if the VIP lowers himself to base humour level, resist the temptation to join in. Maintaining a high degree of decorum at all times will also help you avoid the over-familiarity trap (Covered in Chapter 5).

Empathy and Assertiveness

In this section, I bring empathy and assertiveness together because in a close protection context I would always advocate considering their joint use. Before I expand on this statement it is important to understand exactly what both these words mean. *Empathy* means the power of entering into another's personality and imaginatively experiencing his experiences. Put simply, it is having an emotional identification, and understanding of another person's position or feelings. *Assertiveness* means to declare strongly and to insist upon a particular course of action. Also to be confident, positive, in control and moderately aggressive to achieve an objective. To sum-up this dual approach, it is designed to avoid confrontation and choices for the principal whilst strongly encouraging him to 'buy into your plan'.

A CPO has a unique responsibility to advise and protect the principal (who is directly or indirectly the employer), and yet must always maintain a slightly detached professional working relationship. General security advice given by protection personnel is not always well received as it often works in conflict to the wishes of the principal. Bearing in mind the potential for possible confrontation with the VIP, selecting the right method of communication is of the utmost importance. I advocate that CPO's should address issues at the time of occurrence, as by ignoring them today will encourage their growth to become even bigger problems tomorrow. This 'hot' approach will ensure that the principal recognises your confident assertive style and, although it is unlikely to be welcomed, it will help establish your working parameters.

In the first paragraph of this section I alluded to the fact that assertiveness is a moderately aggressive communication style. If poorly managed there is a risk that this approach to a predicament can be interpreted by the principal as confrontational and aggressive. The protected person feeling that his authority is being threatened or unfairly challenged may over-react by raising his voice and losing his temper. If you respond by also losing your temper, you lose the argument whether you are right or wrong. Remember that ultimately you are the employee (contracted or otherwise), and the adoption of complete control and restraint is of the utmost importance.

Whenever possible I recommend you adopt an *empathetic assertive* approach to difficult issues, as it generally 'softens' the underlying message to encourage principal agreement. This approach basically means recognising the protected persons position or feelings, whilst assertively stating your own needs and requirements. If the principal thinks you are being reasonable and are genuinely empathetic to their position, they will be more likely to agree to your request. A good example of this approach would be when a lengthy motorway road journey precedes an important business meeting set for a particular time. If I became aware of severe delays being experienced on the motorway, I would look at my alternative route plan and adjust the departure time accordingly. This variation in arrangements would have to be discussed with the principal, and I would approach it in the following way; 'Sir, unfortunately there are severe delays on the motorway which will necessitate a change in our travel plans. I know this will be a little inconvenient for you, but we need to leave thirty minutes earlier than originally intended in order to guarantee arrival in time for your second scheduled appointment.'

You can see by the way the above message is delivered that it conveys an apology about the change in arrangements, but clearly states the CP requirements that are necessary to arrive on time. Hopefully the principal will accept your sound advice, but there may be reasons to stick to the original departure time. In these circumstances it is highly likely that the principal will tell you to drive faster or take a short-cut in an attempt to arrive on schedule. The best way to respond to this pressure is to avoid confrontation, and consider a response like: "We will do whatever we can sir". This type of comment conveys a clear signal that you will attempt to reduce the delay, without committing yourself to promises that are unachievable. I would recommend that you make progress on the journey whenever possible, but this must be fully within the speed limits, and always with the utmost safety of the principal, the public and your CP team firmly in the forefront of your mind. Remember your core task in CP is to preserve the life of the principal, so to drive at break-neck speeds to save a few minutes is both reckless and counter-productive. If you achieve the impossible today, you will also be expected to achieve it tomorrow. If in this example you are subsequently late for the second meeting, the principal may unfairly lay the blame on your security arrangements. However, you can be satisfied that you fully communicated the problem to the principal and did everything possible to get him there on time. As a member of a CP team there is a natural desire to always want to achieve your objective, but in these circumstances and having exhausted all your options I strongly suggest you don't lose any sleep over it. As a final guide on this type of issue, one of my golden rules is: 'Generally if the principal leaves late, then they arrive late'.

MEVIN

Excuse me Sir, I know you are enjoying yourself but we should
have left fifteen minutes ago!

The circumstance described in the aforementioned example is a common
problem encountered with virtually all VIP's afforded close protection. As TL
you have to adopt firm policies and strategies to deal with certain issues even
if they are likely to be unpopular with the principal. This delicate subject is
dealt with in depth under 'Incidents and Dilemmas' in Chapter 8.

Communicate Negotiate and Compromise

Communication is integral to dealing with the principal, their family, staff,
colleagues, outside agencies, the public and is often the make-or-break of

CP event planning. The best example of this is during a reconnaissance, when CPO's who are determined to get what they want choose a one-sided approach! This stance can force an intransigent response from other people, when the approach the CPG really needs to adopt is a much more flexible and considerate one. Yes, it is important to have 'Plan A' as your primary objective, but more often than not factors beyond your control force you to consider alternative options.

The most common recce for the CPG to undertake, is a principal's proposed visit to a restaurant. During the planning phase there are certain CP priorities that need to be established. Important first considerations are the table allocated for the VIP and whether the TL can secure a second security table nearby. From a CP perspective the principal's proposed table position may not be ideally situated, and therefore some sort of compromise will need to be negotiated. A tactful approach to the restaurant manager and the use of effective communication skills can often adjust the plan to your preferred option. Negotiation is invariably the key to CP planning, so always maintain a flexible approach to problems and be prepared to reach a compromised solution.

Briefing and Debriefing

Briefing and debriefing are extremely important elements of CP communication, and without them many assignments and events would not run smoothly. Regularly briefing team members of current issues is essential to ensure everyone is informed of on-going developments relating to the principal or a particular task. Thorough handovers from one CP team to another ensures that each team is fully aware of operational issues ensuring a consistent and professional response to the principal at all times. Think of an occasion when as a member of a team you were not briefed properly. You probably experienced feelings of being undervalued, ignored and left in the dark. It is of vital importance to brief team members even if it is only to cover the key points of an assignment. In CP it is common to have insufficient resources, and only limited time to professionally undertake the role as you would like. With such constraints briefing your team takes on a greater importance, as everyone needs to be fully aware of their role to ultimately fulfil the task. Remember a team is only as good as the weakest link.

Many people think that a briefing is always a formal presentation, prepared hours, days or weeks in advance. Within police and military circles, this is often the case, and it is invariably a structured affair that regularly lasts in excess of an hour. In making this statement, I am not being critical of the respective briefing systems, but making an observation of the amount of time, effort and resources available to the police and armed services.

The briefing system that I outline in this book is an adaption of the police system, and fully reflects the needs of the private close protection sector. In CP you generally do not always have the luxury of huge resources and extended time for planning, therefore briefings need to reflect this more realistic position. When you are able to pick your time for a briefing, it is best undertaken when everyone has gathered just prior to an assignment. In this way, you will ensure that the maximum number of people are present, and before starting the task the information will be fresh in everyone's mind.

The purpose of a briefing is to inform, involve and to motivate your audience. The following structure will achieve all these objectives, and if necessary can be shortened to less than one minute. When time is a limiting factor it may be necessary to skip or skim parts of the briefing, so do not feel that every heading has to be covered in detail. The briefing mnemonic that I propose is:

W I I I M A C Q
Welcome
Introduce Self
Information
Intention
Method
Administration
Communications
Questions

Welcome

This part of the briefing is not always necessary, particularly when you are regularly briefing your own team members and there are no outside agencies involved. When new people are present at a briefing, it is important to acknowledge them by name. It commands the individual's attention, values their involvement, and provides an opportunity to introduce them to other team members.

Introduce Self

For similar reasons outlined in the 'Welcome' section above, if you have people in your audience who do not know you it is common courtesy to introduce yourself. It identifies your name and the position you hold within the team, and has the benefit that people can relate to your individual status (i.e. Team Leader).

Information

This should be a succinct overview of all the general information available about the principal and the CP assignment. It must cover detail relating to the length of task, the days and dates involved, timings and the known venues on the itinerary. The threat level should be covered at this stage, supported by any relevant intelligence information as necessary. It is often useful to temporarily hand over to a specialist intelligence officer or colleague for this part of the briefing. If a CP assignment covers a number of days or has a special event included in the planned itinerary, whenever possible I recommend you undertake a separate briefing for each part of the operation.

Intention

Most of this section is obvious, but it would be difficult to outline every intention for every event. I will outline the key points that will apply for most CP assignments:

- To establish and maintain a safe working environment in which a principal can live and work whilst continually minimising risk (Core Task)
- The provision of appropriate and effective Close Protection
- To manage people's access to the principal
- To support partners or other agencies as necessary
- To ensure safety at venues
- To provide immediate first aid facilities
- Provide escape facilities for the principal

Method

The 'Method' is the part of the briefing that contains the majority of information necessary for the CP team to complete the assignment. The team structure would be outlined and individual team roles allocated. Certain individuals undertaking specific tasks may need a more detailed briefing on the method they need to adopt during the assignment. For example there could be specific instructions for the security driver, or a principal's preference on how individuals should be dressed.

Having been briefed on the threat earlier in the briefing, this section should outline the wishes of the principal, particularly relating to overt or covert protective cover. It is extremely important to establish whether the CP team will operate in either a high or low profile way. The method or plan of exactly how the assignment will run should be covered. It should include such points as times and locations of appointments, details of people meeting the principal and arrangements for meals. Primary and secondary routes should be outlined and discussed, and any identified safe havens and designated emergency hospitals. In summary, this section is often the longest part of the briefing, and is where you need to cover every aspect of the task.

Administration

In general terms this section covers support information and material relating to the CP assignment. It may include a briefing note detailing all the important points about the task, which were covered in the formal briefing. Copies of a 'Threat and Risk Assessment' may be provided to team members, with any supporting intelligence material. It is of the utmost importance that the Team Leader or other nominated team member has either the original or a copy of various other CP materials. For example: any maps, route plans, venue plans, hotel booking confirmation, travel tickets, leisure tickets, driving licences and passports. You will note that most of this wish list is shown in plural because wherever possible I always advocate being in possession of a copy of the principal's passport, driving licence and any other tickets and itinerary. Experience has shown that you cannot always rely on the principal to remember all their documentation. Better to be safe than sorry!

Communications

I am going to be a little controversial in this section as so often CP teams consider radios as the number one means of communication. Radios are a very important part of the security package, but on operational close protection they often have restricted use and more importantly limited reception. In restricted use, I mean that the circumstances of CP does not always lend itself to the overt use of radios. It could be that a particular hotel or shop has a ban on their use in public areas, or a venue environment creates specific difficulties for radio transmissions. A music concert and a church service are good examples of events that restrict their use and effectiveness. Covert radio kits with earpieces can be the answer to some of the aforementioned difficulties, but they regularly draw unwanted attention to the principal and also have other limitations. Remember that discreet close protection is often about blending in, and this does not sit well with CPO's overtly displaying or using radios and earpieces. Despite all the above comments, I still advocate the discreet use of personal radios, particularly effective at a residence or on a car-to-car basis.

Undoubtedly the best and most widely used means of communication within CP is a mobile phone. The more expensive handsets can now receive voice, text, e-mail, picture or video messaging with ringtone, discreet, vibrate or silent settings. They can be activated for both national and international use, and have the advantage of being one telephone number for an individual team member at all times. Some problems can be experienced with both network and geographical reception, but in general terms they are perfect for CP and my preferred method of communication.

Mobile phones have the added benefit of being able to store personal telephone numbers, but be cautious not to solely rely on this method for those all-important contact details for hotels, airlines and colleagues. Mobile phones can breakdown, be lost, experience corrupt data, and as one of my friends found when his phone fell into a bucket of water, they are not waterproof. Always back-up your important data and information by another method such as a Palm PC, an organiser or some written record. I favour the old-fashioned method of a notebook and pen, which can contain all the important information I need and is carried in my pocket at all times.

The last point I wish to cover in this section is the use of a Communications Grid. It is a simple colour-coded chart that is an integral part of close protection communications. The use of codes instead of names improves the security of information, and greatly reduces the amount of unnecessary speech over a radio network. Here is a typical example of a Communications Grid:

Communications Grid

Principals (Blue)	Locations (Yellow)	Vehicles (Red)	Routes (Green)	(Brown)	CP Team Names (Grey)
1					
2					
3					
4					
5					

(Colours may be chosen to suit individual requirements)

Questions

At the end of any briefing an opportunity for your audience to ask questions should always be offered. No matter how well you prepare for a briefing, it is easy to overlook points that need to be addressed. During the briefing your CP team will focus on their specific areas of responsibility, and therefore if you omit to cover something in the formal input, they will ask for clarification during this questions session. This discussion period may well highlight new important points, and also allows you as the presenter to check your audience's understanding of the briefing. This is best achieved by asking individuals specific questions relating to their role and responsibilities. In relation to this last point there is a minor risk that by asking your team too many questions, you may transmit a message of your lack of trust in their professional ability.

Debriefing

Debriefing is an element of a CP operation that is often ignored. Whenever possible I would always recommend spending at least a few minutes actively seeking 'hot feedback' from your team members. A debriefing can be as short or as long as you like, but if you do not ask for feedback you certainly won't get it. It needs to be at the conclusion of an event when issues are fresh and clear in everyone's minds. The principle reasons to complete this process are to evaluate the event, highlight any good points and lastly identify areas for improvement. This is one of the best opportunities to praise good work within your team, and although adults tend not to admit it they genuinely like their efforts to be acknowledged. This whole process enhances professionalism, and ultimately promotes and spreads best practice of close protection.

Presentations and Public Speaking

New members of a CP team do not normally conduct presentations or speak publicly, but as you gain experience and seniority, you are likely to be required to lead a more formal presentation or speak to a wider audience.

Before undertaking either of these particular tasks, it is worth re-visiting some parts of this book that provide guidance on how to project the right image and communication messages. In the next few pages I outline some basic guidance on how to achieve a satisfactory performance during any briefing, talk or presentation. If you wish to study the subject matter in more depth, I would recommend you source a professional communication publication available at any library or quality bookshop.

My Advice

For the beginner any event requiring a formal speech to others can be a nerve-racking or terrifying experience. Even for the seasoned professional or regular speaker, a talk on something outside their normal presentation area or comfort zone can occasionally catch them out and generate a bout of unexpected nerves. Public speaking or presentations can take many different forms, but ultimately they are all about performing in front of other people and conveying some sort of message. That message can be very specific like the details of a task or the provision of services, but what is equally important is the presenter. The message starts from the moment an audience sets eyes on you as the speaker. They will immediately form opinions about your appearance, dress, facial expressions and other non-verbal signals long before you have a chance to open your mouth. If you present the wrong image before you start speaking, you will be on an uphill struggle to regain ground.

All speeches or presentations need a structure. After initial introductions they should start with an opening or introduction, a body where most of the presentation is given and finally a conclusion. There are different methods that you may adopt to achieve this, where your talk moves from the experiences of the past, to the present situation and finally to the options for the future. If this approach is not quite applicable it may be better to identify problems with your subject, and then propose or provide suitable solutions. Whatever you do in your presentation ensure you keep it simple and focus on an appropriate opening, a body and a close.

The main purpose of any presentation is to inform, to entertain, even if only to a small degree, and to persuade your audience about a particular topic. Ultimately the key to success is to thoroughly prepare your subject matter, with enough research to gather all the necessary facts. The importance of preparation cannot be over-emphasised. The more you practice and rehearse your presentation, the more confident and relaxed you will become.

In addition to preparing your actual presentation, it is equally important to ensure the venue you have chosen is also fully prepared and functional. On the day of the actual presentation it is crucial to arrive early, to personally check and set-up all the necessary facilities. This early venue preparation will enhance your confidence whilst minimising the opportunities for technical problems beyond your control. It may be the seating layout, the position of the microphone or lighting arrangements, but as I constantly say to people, you must be prepared or you must be prepared to fail.

When a speaker delivers their actual presentation one of the most common mistakes is a tendency to read a speech or notes. This style transmits a message of falseness, poor preparation and can identify you as someone who has limited knowledge of the subject matter. More importantly, it can be incredibly boring - which is the last thing you want to be when talking to a captive audience. It is far better to talk from headings or bullet points and just be as natural as possible. Thorough preparation will negate the need to read anything, and bullet points will ensure you follow your planned presentation structure. Try to maintain good eye contact with as many people in your audience as possible. By not reading your speech it allows you to be spontaneous with your topic, connecting with your audience from the outset. In this way they will all feel fully included in the presentation, and give the impression you are speaking to each one of them personally.

To summarise, good speaking or making a formal presentation is basically good conversation on your feet. Being well prepared will undoubtedly make you more confident, resulting in a more relaxed presentation delivery and allow your topic to flow naturally.

5 THE PRINCIPAL

In my introduction to this book I stressed the importance of the professional working relationship between a principal and all security staff, particularly CPOs. Although security provided by a Residence Security Team (RST) is a very important element of the overall protection package, in this Chapter I focus on the Close Protection Group (CPG) and their professional association with the principal. This relationship is an extremely important element of the job, and is particularly relevant to the person undertaking the role of team leader who has the closest contact with the protected person.

Many principals view close protection afforded by members of the CPG as an invasion of privacy, intent on controlling their every move. The presence of protection around a VIP is often 'suffered' in order to reap the benefits of enhanced safety and privacy afforded by the various cordons of security. If the truth were known, most protected persons do not want to be surrounded by close protection personnel, but circumstances often dictate that they have no option but to suffer it. A sensitive approach to the role will generally win over the principal's approval to accept the presence of personal security. With this in mind, a golden rule you must adopt is to 'Give the principal space whenever possible'.

In initially describing the importance of the relationship with the principal, this closeness must also embrace any contact with the protected person's family and employed staff. It is as important to get on well with other family members and staff as it is to have an alliance with the principal. The upstairs downstairs elements of a VIP's household can be a mix of friendships, sufferance, jealousies and egos. The principal's family, particularly their children and close staff, can be extremely influential in your continuing acceptance by the protected person.

If you reflect on your own personal lives you will know how divisive any breakdown between family members can be. If you upset a principal it *may* affect your continuing employment, but if you also upset the principal's family and staff I would suggest it *will* affect your continuing employment. Some people take great delight in criticising others behind their back, particularly when they are jealous of your closeness and 'chemistry' with the principal. In order to achieve a good working relationship with everyone in a household, I would strongly advise you to just be yourself, and keep out of family and staff politics.

The Over-Familiarity Trap

If like me you are fortunate to work as a PPO in a principal's household for a very long period of time, one situation that is highly likely to confront you will be the temptations of the over-familiarity trap. It would be impossible for me to detail every scenario that reflects stepping over-the-line from a professional relationship with your principal to an over-familiar one. It may be treating their friends like your own, or socialising with them without a formal or implied invitation. Whatever the situation, your judgement needs to be ruthlessly professional at all times. If anything, you should go out of your way to distance yourself from the principal whenever circumstances allow.

A good example of this sort of scenario would be when the protected person visits friends at a private location. All members of the CPG should take this opportunity to keep out of the way, and with a larger CP team some should be sent away to return later. You shouldn't need to wait for the principal to tell you to adopt this approach; better to establish an approximate departure time and make your own judgement. Ultimately the principal will appreciate your

discretion, and it will further develop the chemistry between you.

To explain my own feelings about this sort of situation you need to understand a little about my upbringing and background. My parents were not wealthy and there were times when their joint income was hardly enough to make financial ends meet. I was educated to secondary school level prior to joining the MPCC and ultimately the Metropolitan Police. I spent eight years on uniform duty and had started on the promotional ladder when I joined Royalty Protection. The only reason I was able to take up this appointment was because the Commissioner of the Metropolitan Police had a national responsibility to protect the British Royal Family.

In partnership with other similarly employed officers, that responsibility was ultimately delegated to me during my periods of time on duty. Coming from a fairly humble family background it would have been easy to be overawed and swept along by the situation. Extensive international travel, regularly staying in hotels, driving expensive motor vehicles and visiting special venues were an everyday occurrence. It was of the utmost importance to constantly keep my feet firmly on the ground, and remember that at the end of the day I was a police officer undertaking an official job. I like to think I was always ruthlessly professional in my approach to the role, and when confronted with difficult situations the decisions I made were sound and based on good judgement. A

weaker person could easily have been swept away by circumstances and got drawn into the unprofessional world of the over-familiarity trap. Once snared it is very difficult to withdraw from a situation, and eventually leads to the parting of the ways.

In the private security industry there are also many tempting opportunities for a CPO to advance beyond his primary role of close protection. It is of the utmost importance to stop short of stepping over-the-line, as getting away with something today could well become an issue or dilemma tomorrow. There may be situations where you may think that you are part of the protected person's inner circle, but my advice is that being welcomed into one situation does not mean that you will be included in them all. Another temptation that can occasionally confront a PPO, is directing what the principal does by being selfish and overly assertive. This situation can lead to telling the principal what to do or where to go.

As a TL it is always best to acknowledge the principal's inherent right to make their own decisions about whom they associate with and their planned itinerary. There is however a strong case for a protection operative to give professional security advice or an opinion about a particular situation or venue. This advice must be unbiased and supported by a balanced argument highlighting the relevant options available to the protected person. At the end of the day it is their decision about how their life is conducted, and it only becomes yours when there are serious security issues to consider. Remember that close protection is all about managing risk, and not dictating the principal's movements for personal or selfish reasons.

The Wishes of the Principal

The importance of the wishes of the principal can never be underestimated. At the end of the day close protection can only be achieved by consent. CP is often accepted or suffered by the protected person, because the circumstance of their particular situation merits the need for someone to look after them. It is quite common for the wishes of the principal to work against the specific needs of the close protection team. To take an inflexible and intransigent approach to the provision of CP and in particular the protected person's views, is a highly risky strategy to adopt. Unless your principal is very sympathetic and understanding to this confrontational approach, it will set you on a collision course guaranteed to result in your self-destruction. In the private close protection sector it is equally important to establish your position with the principal. Setting out parameters at any early stage is a very important thing to do, so that both you and the protected person have a clear understanding of the working relationship.

One of my early experiences of valuing the wishes of the principal was in 1981. Together with a few other Royalty Protection Officers I spent short periods of time as a temporary PPO to Lady Diana Spencer. It was shortly after her engagement to HRH The Prince of Wales when the media attention on her and the forthcoming royal marriage was intense. As Personal Protection Officers were a completely new addition and experience in Diana's life, it was of the utmost importance to adopt a discreet yet appropriate approach to the provision of CP. In undertaking this PPO role my security message was simple: "carry on as normal and I will provide appropriate protection around your plans as necessary". If any other PPO or I was concerned about anything, he could still raise the issue and ultimately discuss a compromise solution. This approach acknowledges the principal's position as being in control of their own life, but as deemed necessary allows an opportunity for the PPO to speak and discuss any areas of security concern.

Conversations

In Chapter 4 I provided general guidance on the type of approach and amount of conversation that you should adopt with a principal. You must never lie, don't waffle and avoid discussing politics or religion whenever possible. These subjects can be highly emotive areas of conversation and handled insensitively could alienate you from the protected person. Despite a twenty-first century era of political correctness and potential litigation at every corner, some principals pay scant regard to modern employment law, equal opportunities and the different types of discrimination. It has been known for a CPO to upset a protected person or their family and be removed from a protection assignment for the most trivial of issues. The longer you work with a principal the more trusted you become, often resulting in minor errors or operational mistakes being grudgingly accepted. Over time, as the VIP accepts your integral protection presence, general conversations are likely to become more frequent.

When in conversation with the principal you must always be extremely conscious of a balanced response, your choice of words and the specific tone of delivery. This may appear to be an odd statement to make, but you want to make sure that the message you put across is both the right one and received in the right way. The use of particular emphasis or intonation in speech can infer a completely different meaning to your chosen words. As an example, if you were to say "Good morning" to someone in a smiling and jovial manner, it would transmit a completely different message to someone who says the same thing with a long face and a monotone voice. The latter response transmits a message of disinterest, boredom and just going through the motions of replying. A person who regularly 'puts their foot in their mouth', does not think through their choice of words and is often insensitive to another person's position and values.

Although I have said that you must not lie to the principal, there are occasions when it is best to be a little conservative with the truth and not share everything with them. Some CPOs feel a need to tell the principal absolutely everything about themselves or the protection arrangements. This can be very boring for the principal as they are probably not really interested in a full breakdown of your family tree, or the detailed CP arrangements for their next business meeting. Outlining all your security arrangements can also be counter-productive, particularly when the plans do not work out as you intended. Even the best-laid plans do occasionally go wrong, so if you have shared everything with your principal you will look less than professional when it doesn't come together.

In my experience it is best not to tell the principal everything unless there is a very good reason to do so. "Are they really interested in how many CPO's are in the SAP or that the arrival arrangements are not quite as agreed?" I think it unlikely! Keep any itinerary developments to yourself unless the principal needs to know, specifically asks or is likely to be adversely affected by the plan.

When undertaking the role of a TL, equally important areas of conversation are those that you are not directly involved in but cannot avoid overhearing. Simply by being in close proximity to the principal you will undoubtedly hear private discussions, but you must not overtly listen to them. They may be directly between two or more people present with the VIP, or more commonly during a conversation on a mobile phone. If this situation occurs and the opportunity to move away out of earshot presents itself, then don't wait to be asked - just take the initiative and give the principal space. He will appreciate your awareness of the situation and respect your approach to his privacy. If asked your opinion on something discussed in your principal's 'private' conversation, better to say that you weren't paying attention to his private discussion and didn't hear anything. It may be an integrity test!

Blending In

I have covered the need for a CPO to wear suitable and similar clothing as the principal, in order to blend into any group of people around him. What I have not covered is the art of being an ever-present effective CPO, and yet have the ability to not stand out or be that obvious. By the very nature of the job you cannot 'hide' from the principal or public. With good all-round awareness of a changing situation you can adjust your positioning to be more anonymous as *the grey man or woman*. Knowing when to close in or move away from a principal comes with experience. It would be impossible to detail every CP scenario and outline where a CPO should position himself. More often than not good judgement will lead you to the right solution. I often say that if you think you are in the wrong place then you probably are. As a general guide, the time to be either close or slightly detached from the principal, can basically be narrowed down into two distinct situations:

- Events in a Public Place
- Private Events

Events in a Public Place

In the 100% Safe Chapter you will now have an appreciation of the specific situations that are historically high-risk times. Hopefully you will also have noted that these times are all at public locations where an attacker can predict the principal will eventually appear: home, work, on a regular route, at a public event, or being present at a venue where publicity has been given to your principal's attendance. In these circumstances and particularly in a crowded environment, you are best to be closest to the principal, preferably walking to one side and just behind them. It is worth repeating that historically these situations are when the principal is at their most vulnerable and merits all CPOs to be at their highest state of alertness.

Private Events

Without being complacent, unpublicised events at private locations are the CPO's opportunity to give the principal much needed space and keep out of their way. Provided no publicity has been given to your principal's presence you can be more relaxed in the knowledge that if no one knows they are there the risk must be lower. The word 'relaxed' does not mean 'switched off', but should be interpreted as taking a more detached position whilst still continuing to monitor the situation. Even though the principal is present at a private event he may still need your assistance. He may become the innocent victim of an everyday incident or accident necessitating some form of CP response. You can see therefore that you still need to be contactable and available, but not visually obvious or necessarily in the actual company of the principal.

Over Protection

Over protecting a principal is a cardinal sin, guaranteed to upset your charge. For newly trained CPOs it is one of the most common errors to make, probably because of an unfounded fear of something happening during early CP assignments. Inexperience and nerves contribute to this and are a potentially damaging combination for a CPO. If a principal is someone who has experience of CP, they are highly likely to identify your nervous non-verbal signals at an early stage. When on-duty you must learn to relax; if you cannot, you must give the principal and everyone around them the impression that you are relaxed. A confident calm exterior can hide your much more nervous feelings manifesting themselves inside.

As a guide it may be useful to provide you with a short list of the more common scenarios that can give the protected person the impression that you are over-protecting them:

- Always being too close
- Constantly unnecessarily moving people away from the principal to create space around them
- Overly fussing the principal such as telling them where to cross a road or when the 'Green Man' is lit at a pedestrian crossing
- Unnecessarily updating the principal on all the protection arrangements
- Unnecessarily updating the CPG on the principal's location
- Unnecessary use of a radio or mobile phone
- Unnecessarily touching the principal's arm, back or other parts of their body to guide them through crowded situations
- Standing next to them in shop queues
- Over reacting to innocent people approaching the principal
- Unnecessary use of force against members of the public, particularly if it is likely to adversely affect the principal's image

This list is by no means exhaustive but over protection of a principal is something you must avoid at all costs. Even if you were to provide a less than adequate CP cover, which I do not advocate, this more casual approach would be far less likely to offend the principal. He would probably form the view that you are a very relaxed CPO, in total control and with no obvious security concerns. Most principals are unable to correctly identify effective and appropriate protection anyway! Remember that close protection is all about managing the risk and not eliminating it, so you don't have to be close or physically in the presence of the principal all the time.

6 PRO-ACTIVE PLANNING

Pro-active planning is one of the crucial areas of protective security that the modern professional CPO must embrace and master. In the private security industry it is often the case that a protection team is working within a limited budget and finite resources. Without the benefit of a large close protection team, the importance of being a pro-active CPO who anticipates issues and plans out problems becomes ever more crucial.

In accepting the responsibility of close protection, a CPO should take a leading part in the day-to-day management of a principal's private and business itinerary. In the United States this responsibility has been taken one-step further where the role of the Secret Service has been written into the American Constitution. This provides them with strong powers to enforce their protection arrangements. This is not the case in the UK and particularly CP in the private sector, which is ultimately undertaken with the consent of the principal. Some CP personnel take the view that they want very little involvement with arranging the principal's itinerary, and there is a strong case to argue that this role is the primary responsibility of the VIP's personal staff.

Operationally, it is impossible to separate a principal's daily programme from any close protection arrangements. The two are intrinsically linked and go hand-in-hand together. The security arrangements flow completely through an event from beginning to end, and therefore quite naturally the needs of protection tend to have the biggest influence over a protected person's programme. If a team leader chooses to take a detached position over the principal's itinerary he will quite understandably be left out of any arrangements made. Knowledge is power, and wherever possible, my strong recommendation would be to take a keen interest in the principal's programme so as to have both input and influence over the itinerary from the outset.

In close protection one of the most important stages of pro-active planning is the reconnaissance phase. A reconnaissance is basically a preliminary survey of a venue or place and is better known by the abbreviated military term 'recce'. The basic purpose of a protective recce is to explore all considerations when planning an event and make appropriate close protection decisions based on your findings. There are basically only two types of reconnaissance:

- An overt reconnaissance is one undertaken without the need for secrecy, mainly appropriate for public events or events in a public place that have received prior publicity.

- A covert reconnaissance is one undertaken in secret or when discreetly visiting a venue to plan a protection operation without necessarily revealing the identity of the principal.

I cannot stress strongly enough the importance of undertaking a recce as a *must* for any event whenever possible. For a CPO to go blind into a venue is the worst case scenario, so even when time is limited it is better to undertake a hasty recce than to not complete one at all! I can remember many an occasion when having been given very little notice of a protection task, mainly private, stealing a few minutes to undertake a quick recce of a venue enabled me to at least identify the arrival point and a few other key geographical factors. As a team leader, if time or logistics make it impossible to complete a recce yourself, and you have the assistance of a support protection team, you should always consider sending them ahead as a SAP. Without the luxury of other CPOs, the only other option available to you is to telephone ahead to ascertain some key facts and then run with it. This is not an ideal situation, but as most of these occasions are likely to be private events with no publicity at least the risk would be low.

In planning protection assignments it is hugely important to be sympathetic to the needs of other individuals and different organisations that invariably have some sort of input or agenda that can impact on a protected person's programme. Ultimately protection is about a partnership between many different groups of people from the principal at the top, staff members, various organisations, event planners, workers on the day and the CPG. Their interest and influence can vary depending on their status and whether the programme or event is either private or public. Whichever category a principal's itinerary fits into, there are always people who have an agenda which they consider to be just as important as any protection arrangements.

A range of different factors will influence many protection decisions - often completely outside the control of the protection team leader. Examples of these factors are the choice of an event venue, event protocols, reception invitations or whom the principal will meet during an official function. I have stressed several times throughout the book that CP is about managing risk, and unfortunately when planning security events you will not always get your own way. A CP team leader will invariably take the lead on a VIP's itinerary and he must be mindful of not being completely selfish about the security arrangements. This approach can occasionally be achieved with a very senior high-profile VIP at a public event, but with a private sector principal the solution often lies in the CPO's ability to effectively communicate, be flexible and come to a compromise solution acceptable to all parties. One thing I would implore you to take from this Chapter is one of my most important golden rules namely: *time spent on reconnaissance is never wasted.*

At an early stage in the process of operational planning and any subsequent reconnaissance, it is essential to identify the key groups and partners who possess a genuine interest in a principal's itinerary. This interest could be well intentioned or have a more sinister undertone, but in order to make the event work some common ground has to be identified and agreed.

The following individuals or groups may have an interest in a protection event:

The Principal

The principal partner in the whole planning process is the protected person. His wishes are the most important and the obvious ones to satisfy. As this particular point was addressed at some length in the previous Chapter, I will only make one further comment on the subject. The principal's wishes are naturally important in the decision making process, but should not be considered paramount or in 'tablets of stone'. Their individual preferences should be catered for whenever possible, but there are occasions which merit a different approach.

It would be impossible for me to give you examples of every scenario where you will need to make a decision that conflicts with the wishes of your principal. I can only advise that you should only ignore or vary their preferences if you have a very good reason to do so. In these circumstances it is best to inform the protected person of the changed arrangements, and you must always be prepared to justify your decisions. I can guarantee that when the principal learns of your changes of plan not only are they likely to be unpopular, but you will undoubtedly be asked the question "Why?" You need to be in a position to offer an immediate and objective explanation, otherwise you will lose much credibility and appear unprofessional. This strategy can be quite confrontational with a principal, and I would only recommend it when no other options are available to you.

The Principal's Staff

After the principal, his immediate staff is the next group with whom you should strike up a particularly good working relationship. Without their support and co-operation your life could be made extremely difficult. Generally, the principal will employ his staff directly, and their role will be to serve and keep their employer happy at all costs - a very different role to a CPO. Their duties are wide and varied and include managing the principal's personal life as well as his official programme of appointments.

It is vital that you have a good rapport and constant dialogue with all staff members. They have unrivalled access and the immediate ear of the VIP, and can help you enormously with information about the principal's plans and arrangements, particularly any private programme. Sharing general information such as departure times, arrangements for lunch or that unexpected appointment can make your life a whole lot easier.

For an event that is going to be publicised it is important to agree with the protected person's personal staff what information is to be released and when. As a guide, any media statements should only contain general information about the principal and event plans rather than specifics about timings or the itinerary. Unnecessary disclosure of any detailed programme is bad for protective security, and is potentially providing a would-be attacker with all the information they require. An agreed staged release of general information is the best approach, and if any specific details need to be made public then this should be done as near to the event date as possible.

Event planners should particularly avoid publicising the specifics of the route a principal will take, the vehicle he will be travelling in, where he will be seated and any other very personal information. Restricting the circulation of any detailed itinerary to only those who need to know, will be hugely beneficial to the security arrangements. Do not forget that any working partnership must be a two-way process, so it is essential to update the principal's staff on things that directly affect them also.

A good example of this partnership approach would be to inform the chef of a substantial delay in the protected person's return to a residence in time for dinner. The chef can then adjust the principal's meal arrangements so that, for instance food is not overcooked. This sort of assistance will be remembered and a possible advantage for such help is that you will never go hungry again!

As a final point on the principal's immediate staff it is worth reflecting on their potential for influencing others. With the constant ear of the protected person and his immediate family, staff members can be extremely supportive or very destructive to the close protection team. You would be ill advised to be deliberately unhelpful or unwittingly upset members of the VIP's staff. If you are at all rude or not a popular member of the wider team, the undue influence that staff members can have should not be underestimated. You could become the subject of a deliberate or calculated ploy to damage your popularity, character or reputation. It can be very difficult to redress or counter this rear-guard action. Who said life was fair?

Event Organisers

Organisers of events fall into many different categories and their agendas will depend on the specific role the principal has in attending a function. They may be company representatives, professional event managers, volunteers or charity workers. If the principal is attending a function in a private capacity then the interest of event organisers is likely to be minimal or non-existent. Private events tend to be more casually organised affairs, and therefore far easier to adjust the arrangements to suit any CP requirements. If the event is an official one and the protected VIP is attending as the principal guest, then the organiser's agenda will be much more clearly defined. It is likely that they will have certain objectives to fulfill: e.g. to finalise arrangements to open a building, to allocate seating for guests at dinner, to maximise publicity and exposure of the principal. Changing 'official programmes' to better suit the protection arrangements is not an easy task to achieve. However, approached in the right way event organisers are often willing to make adjustments to their planned itinerary. These changes could be things like minor adjustments to timings, reducing the time spent in a reception or changing the arrival point to accommodate security considerations. To achieve programme amendments such as these, good communication and negotiation skills are essential. It is no surprise that yet again we re-visit the importance of interpersonal communication skills highlighted in Chapter 4.

Venue Security

Similar to 'Event Organisers', the approach that venue security adopt towards a protected person will vary considerably. This unpredictable support will depend on the identity of the protected person, the available security resources and the importance that they place on a particular event. The public profile of the principal may well stir some unexpected offer of security assistance, particularly if you were protecting a well-known film celebrity compared to an unknown chairman of a private company. Managed correctly their interest, for whatever motive, may prove to be very helpful to your close protection arrangements. If their approach is to be overly inquisitive or nosey, it may prove to be more of a hindrance than anything else. The worst case scenario is that venue security personnel are completely disinterested in the presence of your principal. However, in the private security industry if money was no object you can always resort to an option to pay for additional security measures.

Official Agencies

Official agencies such as the police rarely have any interest or input into the arrangements surrounding a privately protected person. Occasionally the profile of such an individual may generate an extreme public and media attention that forces official agencies to provide protection assistance. When private protection arrangements overlap with official agencies it tends to be as a direct result of other factors such as public safety or an official attending an event (i.e. A member of the British Royal Family or a Cabinet Minister). When an event is officially managed, private protection personnel are advised to follow any instructions given to them by the police or government representatives. It is worth noting that if you accompany a principal to a private event also attended by an officially protected person (i.e. The Foreign Secretary), you may not be allowed entry into the function. The control of the event rests with both the organisers and police, and you should be aware that when the officially protected person leaves the venue the police protection arrangements would end. After that you are on your own again!

The Public

The public are the most unpredictable and often unknown group of people in the planning process of any close protection equation. Historically they can hide individuals who are a real threat to the protected person, and as alluded to in Chapter 1, statistically account for many direct attacks on VIPs. The vast majority of people who wait outside official function venues or attend as paying guests, are there quite innocently and pose no threat to a principal. There are however some followers of VIPs whose interest borders on the obsessive. This obsession can evolve into a fixation which as a potential stalker can result in threats of violence, serious assault or ultimately assassination.

When faced with enthusiastic crowds, most VIPs particularly members of the British Royal Family and high-profile popular celebrities, only experience the presence of happy, friendly fans. Whilst such a crowd may contain extremist group members or terrorists, you are more likely to have problems with managing their enthusiasm and controlling the sheer weight of the people present than any threatening incident. If you have responsibility or influence over how the crowd is controlled, it is of the utmost importance to plan your crowd control arrangements well in advance of the event. You must undertake a risk assessment of the event, estimating the numbers and put into place proper crowd control measures including substantial barriers that fully comply with all Health and Safety Regulations. Flimsy rope or plastic tape deployed to control members of the public is useless. If you do not designate and professionally control areas where the public may gather, you can be assured that they will stand in all the wrong places and the protection arrangements will be compromised.

If ever there is a key area in CP to be pro-active in planning out potential problems, then the management of all arrangements for a principal's arrival and departure at venues, particularly public ones, is a top priority. Providing an appropriate balance of security staff to 'police' the event is also important, as a crowd overseen by too many security may become less friendly. This friction can develop if large numbers of overt security personnel stand in front of the crowd and make it difficult for the public to see either the VIP or the event. Professionally briefing your security staff about their responsibilities and this potential problem should enable them to monitor the situation, adapt accordingly and avoid any potential conflict.

In the private security industry the presence of a hostile crowd or group is an increasingly more common occurrence. With the drive for a green environment, an abhorrence of hunting and animal experimentation, it is not surprising that groups like Greenpeace and the Animal Liberation Front are so active and have growing support. Providing close protection for a chairman or chief executive of a high-risk company often brings you into conflict with these or similar groups. The presence of a particular VIP may not be the specific reason for a demonstration or hostility, but he may be the vehicle for the oxygen of wider publicity for the group's particular cause.

An excellent example of this strategy was in 2005 and 2006 when the UK 'Fathers For Justice' group demonstrated at Buckingham Palace, Downing Street and the Houses of Parliament. Another targeted event may be a company's Annual General Meeting, or the site of a new but unpopular factory development. In an ideal world it would be the preferred option of the CPG to avoid confrontation with any demonstrators. A plan for the principal to enter via a more discreet or private entrance would be ideal, but often the intransigent wishes of the principal prevent this pro-active approach and draw CPOs into a position of unnecessary risk. It is these exact circumstances that best highlight the importance of good security reconnaissance and pre-planning to preferably avoid, or ultimately manage, a potentially high-risk scenario. Whatever the situation, going blind into this sort of volatile scenario is the last thing you want to be doing. Being a forward thinking CPO and one step ahead of the game is the answer to this sort of predicament!

The Public Risk

We now know that all public areas are potentially high-risk times for security personnel, and that lurking amongst any public group may be someone who is a real threat to the principal. So how do we identify a potential attacker or fixated person from within a group of innocent guests or members of the public? Potential attackers tend to be people who are not acting naturally in any particular environment. By observing people's general behaviour and non-verbal communication signals, there are many tell-tale indicators that can identify an individual who may pose a threat to the principal. Some, or a combination of the following warning signs, may indicate someone who needs to be watched by security personnel:

- Sweating
- Staring
- Wide eyes
- Not smiling
- Frowning
- Quiet demeanour
- Not communicating with people around them
- Wearing unusual clothing for an event
- Wearing too much clothing (concealing a weapon or other items such as a banner or placard)
- Nervous behaviour (agitated or unusual reactions)
- Clenched fists
- Hands hidden from view (may be holding a weapon)
- Unusual movement within a crowd
- Pacing up and down
- Verbal threats
- People positioning themselves where any crowd barrier controls end or where they are at their weakest (by walls or barriers not connected properly)

Rooftop Arrival

It is worth mentioning that many of the detailed warning signs listed are identical to those displayed by people suffering from mental disorder. Their behaviour may be similar to a fixated person and this type of person may be a threat to a principal, but they may also be just a harmless follower with no evil intent whatsoever. The UK Government's 'Care In The Community' policy has increased the number of people with mental disorders being treated in a public community environment. As a result a CPO working with a high-profile celebrity is now much more likely to come into contact with someone suffering from schizophrenia or other mental illness.

If in the worst case scenario someone is planning to attack a principal, they are going to be nervous and unlikely to be acting naturally. As a private CPO you have no legal rights to detain or search anyone whom you think is a threat to you or a protected person. If you observe activity that makes you genuinely worried about someone's motives, then you can talk to them and ask them questions to allay or confirm your concerns. If police are present then advise them of your observations and leave them to deal with the matter. You can then continue to observe the individual and developments until the principal has passed any potential danger.

The Media

The media is one group of people that, whether you like them or hate them, with protected VIPs you cannot escape them! It may surprise you to know that although I have personal experience of both the good and bad side of their role, I have sympathy with their position. I do not agree with some of the more aggressive, immoral or illegal tactics that they regularly employ, but at the end of the day they have a particular task to perform. In general, if they are treated fairly they will respond and behave reasonably.

One thing you must understand about the media is that *nothing* is 'off the record' and there is no such thing as a last photograph. Their agenda is definitely not your agenda, so be wary of them but do not be hostile. It is extremely wise to be careful about what you do or say to the media, particularly in a public environment. Although close protection often brings you into conflict with the press, good working relations can still be achieved by understanding their needs. I do not advocate facilitating whatever the media want, just as I also do not support being deliberately obstructive either.

If the press turn up unannounced at a private event to which they have not been invited, then they take their chances about whether they do or do not get any story or photographs. There is no obligation whatsoever on anyone to provide them with any access or facilities to achieve their objectives. If however the media are personally invited or attend to report on a particular public event, there is a natural and reasonable expectation by them of being provided with enough access and facilities to fulfill their assignment. Constantly taking an aggressive stance with the press is not the answer, as it is far better to keep cool, be relaxed and negotiate a solution acceptable to all. Take a fair and firm approach at all times and be mindful of the fact that they are not the enemy!

Although unlikely to be part of your close protection role it is worth touching on some guidance for media interview techniques, You can learn a lot from the masters of communication who deal with challenging media on a daily basis. Politicians may not be the most popular people in the world, but they are well experienced when it comes to dealing with the press. How often have you seen or heard a politician asked a specific question and they do not answer it directly? That is because they either wish to avoid the subject, or more often than not they have their own agenda that they wish to address.

Just because a member of the media asks you a question does not mean that you have a duty to answer it. As a Royalty Protection Officer I was regularly asked inappropriate questions by the accompanying press, and often I would just ignore it or respond with a question myself. It was a bit like a jousting game where the royal-rota press knew what the protection officers were doing, but they still felt a professional 'duty' to occasionally try and illicit some information that may benefit their role. In the private close protection sector you must be equally cautious of what you say when dealing with the paparazzi. Here are a few guidelines that may give you some strategies for dealing with hostile members of the media:

- Be relaxed and keep cool at all times
- Be fair and firm
- Have your own agenda – at least three points or questions
- You are always on defence not attack
- Never rush into interviews – be prepared
- Never take calls from media you do not know – ring them back
- Assume that everything you say is being recorded
- Anticipate questions, much like a job interview
- With hostile questions do not talk about the problem but answer with some new or powerful facts and solutions
- Be friendly, particularly when the interviewer gets hostile

Planning and Reconnaissance

I have now identified and discussed the key groups and partners who are likely to have some interest and input into the planning and reconnaissance phase of a close protection assignment. The importance of this phase cannot be over-stated in protection terms as by getting it right before the event prevents incidents occurring later. It is no good after an event saying, "I never thought that would have happened", as anticipating problems and reducing risk is a core role of close protection. You must be pro-active and not reactive.

I do not intend to detail every scenario and all the options you should consider when planning out problems, but suffice to say that you must be thinking ahead and very laterally at all times. In communication and conflict management skills training you are constantly being advised about awareness, anticipation and avoidance. In reconnaissance the situation is exactly the same, and time spent in this capacity is never wasted. When planning a close protection assignment the following list will assist in identifying some of the key problem areas:

- If resources allow, deploy an SAP, particularly for a public event
- Select a minimum of two routes to and from the venue
- Identify safe havens en route and at a venue
- Identify a designated hospital (24 hour Accident and Emergency)
- Identify the high-risk times (arrival, departure points, etc)
- If appropriate and acceptable to everyone, consider an alternative entrance or exit
- Reduce the amount of time the principal spends walking to and from any vehicle
- Reduce the amount of time the principal spends in a public area
- Restrict public access to the principal
- Plan designated and barrier areas for enthusiastic or hostile crowds
- Monitor the press, particularly photographers
- Arrange for someone else to manage the media
- Restrict the circulation of any detailed programme of the event to those who need to know only
- Any press release should not show any detailed timings
- Guard the principal and close protection vehicles at all times

Having set out several key guidelines to reconnaissance, I am aware that many of the areas require additional resources that are not always available in the private industry. Cost will always be a deciding factor when planning an event, and, as much importance should be placed on providing an appropriately resourced protection assignment as providing too much. It would be an error to over-resource any security plan by providing an expensive and inappropriate protection 'comfort zone' that is highly likely to annoy the principal and alienate other partners to the event.

Reconnaissance Sheet

I have now outlined how important a recce is in the wider picture of operational planning. The amount of detail that can be dedicated to that task is dependent on many different factors, but particularly available time and resources. On the assumption that as team leader you have been provided with plenty of notice for a public event, contact with key personnel should be made at the earliest opportunity. This contact establishes those first building blocks in creating a partnership for a successful event. In an ideal world it is best to complete a recce some days in advance of the task, but after the principal's programme has been put into draft format.

When undertaking an overt recce it is quite common to be asked views about the security arrangements before you have even had an opportunity to view the venue and consider the plan. It is crucial to 'walk the course' before making any decisions about the final security arrangements. What is written on the event's draft programme may be neither accurate nor workable. By reviewing the draft plan and itinerary first, you will be better informed to make decisions for the benefit of everyone. This can be a difficult balancing act to achieve, but getting it right at the planning stage is often the key to a successful problem-free visit for all parties.

In the next few pages a 'Reconnaissance Sheet' is detailed as an aide-memoire to planning a simple event or close protection assignment. It is not intended that this sheet is used for every protection recce but where there is ample time for effective planning, this is a good template report form to guide you through the key areas for consideration. The document is not designed for use by Security Consultants in detailed security audits, and does not cover *every* consideration for a particular task. The headings on the sheet are basic, but adequate to cover most protection events, and in sufficient detail to prepare a formal presentation or team briefing pack. In the private close protection sector the reality is that if you are using this form to prepare a formal CP team briefing then you have probably achieved utopia.

Threat

Reconnaissance Sheet

Day & Date	
Event	
Dress Code	
Venue	

Timings	Depart To Venue	Arrive at Venue	Depart from Venue

Organiser	Contact at Venue	Recce Date

Tel No	Tel No	Recce Time

Vehicle Transport

Motor Vehicle	Index No	Driver	Supplier

Vehicle Security

Other Transport

Mode of Transport				
Name of Carrier				
Company Contact	Ticket Arrangements	Departure Arrangements	Arrival Arrangements	

Route

Basic Route Details
Primary
Secondary

Communications

Radio Channel(s)		Call Sign(s)	
Close Protection Team Details (Name / Mobile Tel / Role)			

Principal's Accommodation

Location	
Telephone No	
Contact at Location	

	Room No / Name	Telephone No	Notes
Principal's Room			
Close Protection Room(s)			
Other Security Arrangements			

Designated Hospital		
Name	Address	Telephone No

Other Security Considerations

Issues	Yes	No	Details
Physical Search			
Electronic Search			
Dog Search			
Safe Haven			
Exits / Alarms			
Toilets			
Control of Access Guests / Public			
Searching Bags & Guests			
Screening of Gifts / Flowers			
Media Arrangements			
Close Protection Meal Arrangements			

Notes

7 INCIDENTS AND DILEMMAS

Incidents and dilemmas are unplanned situations or predicaments that can occasionally occur within a close protection environment. What is unusual about these issues is that historically it is one of the few areas of CP that the vast majority of CPOs will have received little or no formal guidance or training. Conversely, from a team's perspective it is an area that can affect an operational CPO on a regular basis. It may be an everyday problem like a traffic delay, or a more difficult situation like the principal committing a crime. Whatever the situation, a CPO must maintain a flexible approach and needs coping strategies to manage unexpected or challenging scenarios.

As an instructor in a classroom environment 'Incidents and Dilemmas' can be a highly emotive subject to facilitate. Sessions regularly result in students adopting different and occasionally opposing solutions to problems. Even the Directing Staff (DS) occasionally find it difficult to provide students with the definitive answer to a particular scenario. In many cases different strategies can arguably all be an appropriate response to a predicament, and it is often just a matter of a CPO making a reasoned judgement that ultimately resolves the issue. As you read this Chapter, one clear message that I would like you to absorb is that there is more than one way to resolve an issue and *all* the potential options could be right!

Incidents

In this section I define some typical incidents that can occur whilst being employed in a protection role. Incidents can best be described as day-to-day occurrences that require some sort of professional response or solution. It would be impossible to provide you with a complete list of all the different situations that a CPO may find himself involved with, so I have listed the more common or likely occurrences:

- An aircraft delay
- An aircraft the principal is travelling in is diverted to a different airport
- A Road Traffic Accident (RTA) involving the principal
- A sudden death in the principal's family

- A TL / PPO / CPO is injured on-duty
- A TL / PPO / CPO becomes ill whilst on-duty
- The principal wants to stop and provide assistance at an RTA
- Severe traffic delays
- The back-up protection vehicle suffers a mechanical breakdown
- The CPG have insufficient time to undertake a reconnaissance
- The media are very intrusive
- The media swamp the principal
- The primary route is blocked (fatal RTA, flooding, police incident, etc)
- The principal collapses
- The principal has a domestic crisis
- The principal is driving and gets stopped by the police
- The principal is surrounded by enthusiastic fans
- The principal is taken ill
- The principal mistakenly gets into the wrong vehicle
- The principal suffers some sort of personal injury
- The principal's vehicle suffers a mechanical breakdown
- The principal's vehicle suffers a puncture
- The principal's vehicle sustains a broken windscreen
- The principal witnesses a crime (fail to stop RTA, robbery, theft, etc)
- You confront an intruder on the principal's property

Solutions to many of these incidents are clear cut and relatively easy. In the event of transport disruption, choosing an alternative route or mode of transport may be all that is required to solve the problem. If the principal's vehicle suffered a mechanical breakdown, the amount of available CP resources may lead you to the right answer. If you had the luxury of a following back-up car, then the obvious solution would be to transfer the principal into that vehicle and continue with his journey. The driver or a CPO would be left with the principal's vehicle to maintain security and ultimately resolve the problem. If you didn't have the luxury of a supporting back-up vehicle, then the solution may depend on the wishes of the principal. Time may be critical so a taxi could be the answer, or the principal may be happy to limp the vehicle to a local garage and wait whilst immediate repairs are completed. The latter option would not be a high-risk situation or compromise the protection arrangements because nobody, not even the CPG, could have predicted that the principal would stop at a random garage for emergency vehicle repairs.

At a public event another common occurrence is when the media or over-enthusiastic fans swamp a high-profile celebrity. This sort of incident can be far more difficult to manage, because the natural CP response in this situation would be to provide body cover and evacuate the principal. Often it is not as simple as that because there are many other factors to consider, such as the public profile, image and wishes of the principal. With the media in attendance any action taken by the CPG will be recorded, analysed, scrutinised and potentially reported in both the newspapers and on television.

The VIP may not welcome an overbearing approach by CPOs, and any actual physical contact with the media or public must be within the constraints of English Law. Very often closing in around the principal is the correct first response, followed by a fair, firm assertive use of verbal communication skills to negotiate your way through a crowd. Putting hands on someone to move them away or aside is technically an assault, however an assault is justifiable in law when defending yourself and others provided you use no more force than is necessary and it is reasonable and justifiable in the circumstances. Each situation would be dealt with on its merits, but putting hands on someone should always be a last resort!

At some point during a CP assignment you and your principal will drive past, witness or more worryingly are involved in a road traffic accident. As a CPO your priority will always be to preserve the life of the principal, and ultimately keep them away from any potential danger. This danger naturally includes such things as every-day motor vehicle accidents. This is a relatively common incident where the wishes of the principal are highly likely to oppose your natural protection instincts. You will want to keep them away from the incident, and they will want you to stop and offer some sort of help! Whether you like it or not, the VIP's understandable human response to another person's 'cry for help', is likely to be so strong that you are best advised to follow their wishes. It may be just to offer some reassuring words of comfort whilst waiting for emergency assistance, or it could involve more tangible help like administering first-aid treatment. But, you can just imagine the vitriolic media criticism if it became public knowledge that a protected person ignored a RTA and drove past injured people in need of help. If as the PPO you chose to ignore the accident against the principal's wishes, potentially it could seriously effect your security of tenure and would undoubtedly be a bad thing for the principal's image.

Dilemmas

What is a dilemma? Basically it is a predicament or difficult situation that anyone can find themselves in. The broader dictionary definition of 'dilemma' describes it as a mire which is further defined as a swamp, bog, ooze or mud. Bearing in mind the closeness of CPOs with their principals, these words accurately describe the sticky situations that a CPO can be confronted with.

Dilemmas come in many different disguises and they can hide amongst a broad spectrum of issues that can be ethical, cultural, philosophical or the more obvious criminal. To the untrained or less scrupulous person, an evolving dilemma can be quite difficult to identify. They are not always as obvious as the principal committing a crime, but could be an inappropriate relationship developing beyond the professional role you should maintain. It could be unsolvable cultural differences between a TL and his principal or personal difficulties surrounding the protected person's extended family. The real key to dealing with these challenging problems is having an open mind to different solutions, properly supported by some pre-prepared coping strategies. Before I propose potential solutions to evolving predicaments, let me identify many of the more common close protection dilemmas:

- You witness the principal assaulting a member of the public
- Whilst on duty the principal offers to buy you an alcoholic drink
- You witness or are aware that the principal has committed a criminal offence
- Whilst driving a motor vehicle the principal commits a road traffic offence
- The principal is 'obviously' drunk and attempts to drive a motor vehicle
- The principal commits adultery or cheats on their partner
- The media attempt to bribe you for information
- The principal asks you to 'set up' the media for publicity purposes
- The principal seeks your advice on personal or family matters
- You don't like the principal and/or their family
- You don't like the principal's pets
- The principal is regularly drunk
- The principal indulges in the services of prostitutes
- You are asked to pick up prostitutes for the principal
- The principal is constantly aggressive towards you (shouting and swearing)
- The principal partakes of illegal drugs
- The principal behaves inappropriately to you or others (crude, sexism, racism)
- The principal constantly asks you for personal favours (shopping, gardening, etc)
- The principal constantly treats you like a servant (washing cars, walking the dog, carrying shopping, etc)
- You find yourself becoming over-familiar with the principal
- You find yourself being seduced by the principal's lifestyle (living the high life)

- Your CP role adversely affects your home circumstances (family pressures)
- Friends and colleagues ask you indiscreet questions about your principal
- A member of your team is unfit for duty due to excess alcohol
- A member of your CP team is witnessed taking illegal drugs
- Unauthorised use of the principal's transport by a CP team member
- You are sexually attracted to the principal
- You have an inappropriate sexual relationship with the principal
- You experience a conflict of values and/or beliefs with the principal
- The principal asks to be left alone at an unknown location
- The principal keeps trying to lose you and/or the CP team
- The principal tells you to go away and leave him or her alone
- The principal tells you to travel in the back-up car
- The principal or their partner asks you about the activities of the other
- You are asked to disclose confidential information or issues of a sensitive nature
- You accidentally lose some of the principal's money or property
- You are involved in a RTA whilst driving the principal's motor vehicle
- You are offered generous gratuities which may be a bribe
- The principal asks you to join him or her at private social events (dinner parties, etc)
- You experience a conflict between duty to your 'client' and duty to the 'principal'
- The principal does not share necessary information with you (being shut out)
- You experience aggression towards your principal (may be due to other factors)
- You experience personal feelings of dislike towards your principal
- You violently disagree with the principal's political views
- You dislike the principal's sexuality
- You experience a personality clash with the principal
- You experience wide cultural differences with the principal that you cannot come to terms with

Management and Solutions

The vast majority of people who work within the UK private close protection circuit are self-employed. CP assignments can be offered and accepted at very short notice, therefore time available to undertake any research on your future charge can be limited or non-existent. If time allows it is always best to confidentially profile your principal, much like you would a formal threat and risk assessment. Particular attention should be made to identify the principal's political, religious, family and cultural background. Consideration must be given to how their personal values may impinge on both your values and the sheer mechanics of providing appropriate CP. Information gathered may identify areas of potential difficulty or conflict, which you as the CPO should be mindful of and sensitive in your approach to managing the problem. Even if you cannot identify any potential areas of conflict or difficulty with the principal, the most innocent of scenarios can quickly develop into a predicament. I strongly advise all members of the CPG to be well prepared for a possible dilemma, and always be ready with a range of suitable coping strategies.

I do apologise for interrupting you sir, but I heard strange noises and thought there may be an intruder!

Although the protected person is not always the employer, I acknowledge that their position carries tremendous influence and power. It is natural for all private industry CPOs to be concerned about retaining their particular job or contract and not upsetting the principal. Naturally it is far easier for a CPO to just 'go with the flow', and not risk the wrath of their principal in the hope that nothing untoward occurs. My honestly held belief is that a protected person is directly or indirectly employing you to both preserve their life but also to provide them with a professional service that includes security advice. The vast majority of protected persons do not want a servant-like, sycophantic weak-willed individual who will always say "Yes" to them at every opportunity. Most principals prefer to employ an honest close protection operative who will provide sound professional advice, even if it is potentially confrontational or controversial. Remember a very good professional CPO knows when to say "No" and if necessary can always justify their decisions.

Coping Strategies

The final part of this Chapter deals with coping strategies as the CPOs professional options for potential solutions to a particular dilemma. Some of these coping strategies are best described as negative responses to the problem such as doing nothing and continuing to monitor the evolving situation. Other coping strategies are longer-term solutions like talking to the principal over time and asserting your influence over their inappropriate behaviour or lifestyle. Another successful strategy is to confidentially discuss the issue with a security supervisor or other members of your team. I accept that there are certain dilemmas and situations where it would be completely inappropriate to share any details with a friend or colleague. However, with smaller less controversial issues I advocate you give serious consideration to discussing them with other team members, particularly those with a lot of CP experience. This approach will share the dilemma by combining two minds, and sharing a problem is often halving it.

You may well find that your colleagues have also experienced the same or a similar predicament, and have either resolved or are actively managing the problem. Sharing the dilemma will also provide you with an opportunity to agree with other members of your team a specific unified coping strategy. This will ensure a professional and consistent response to the principal at all times. This approach tackles the potentially difficult area of a principal questioning different team members and playing one member off against another. The issues may be relatively small such as vehicle routes or journey timings, but the size of the issue is unimportant compared to the team response. If your strategy is for all team members to provide the same answer to the principal, then he is much more likely to quietly accept your collective advice and leave the issue alone.

The final and ultimate coping strategy is to decide to resort to legal proceedings by reporting the principal and the incident or dilemma to the police. It is often suggested to me that this situation would never arise, particularly as a CPO involved would be breaching confidentiality and would potentially never work in the private CP sector again. The latter may well be true, but I believe that everyone has a limit to their loyalty and that certain criminal offences by your principal would merit the ultimate response. Apart from your own moral standards and an individual's legal obligations to report serious crime, I will leave you to consider the following question: Would you remain silent about your principal's involvement in murder or sexual offences involving children?

It is no co-incidence that many of the following coping strategies are inherently linked to an individual's ability to communicate effectively. The various options all involve the softer skills such as talking to the principal, speaking to colleagues, providing well-informed advice over a period of time, assertiveness, listening or just monitoring a situation. Whatever strategy you adopt, being well prepared with an immediate response will provide you with a confidence to effectively manage the dilemma.

The following is not the definitive list of coping strategies, but it will provide you with a wide selection of options when deciding how to address your predicament:

1. Listen to experienced advice during your formal close protection training.
2. Be prepared with a professional plan and response for the principal if an incident or dilemma develops.
3. Be aware of the principal's political, cultural, religious and personal circumstances.
4. Be aware of the principal's own values.
5. Do nothing.
6. Monitor the situation and see how it develops.
7. Talk to the principal about the incident or dilemma. This could be at the time of the predicament or over a longer period of time (the drip-drip method). *(Remember – principals are only human and often more approachable than you think!)*

8. Use *'empathetic assertiveness'* communication skills.

9. Confidentially discuss the issue with a member of the principal's family or staff. This option is particularly applicable when the principal is a juvenile and the client is the parent or guardian. *(Warning - this can be a very risky strategy particularly in maintaining a good professional relationship with your principal!)*

10. Seek advice by sharing the incident or dilemma with an experienced Close Protection colleague or mentor.

11. Seek advice by sharing the incident or dilemma with a close personal friend, but be acutely aware of maintaining the utmost confidentiality.

12. Report the incident or dilemma to a Close Protection supervisor.

13. In extreme cases you could consider a move to another Close Protection assignment. With this chosen option you must also consider whether you are just 'ducking the issue', leaving the dilemma for someone else to manage and resolve.

14. The ultimate coping strategy is to decide to resort to legal proceedings by reporting the principal and the incident or dilemma to the police. In this case you are highly likely to be asked to make a written statement, and must if necessary be prepared to go to court and give evidence for the prosecution. If in the circumstances you do not voluntarily leave your current CP position, you must expect to be dismissed or be asked to leave immediately.

Conclusion

In considering the various coping strategies, it is important to bear in mind that a dilemma for one CPO is not necessarily a dilemma for another. A dilemma for a CPO is not necessarily a dilemma for a principal. Whatever your chosen strategy and response to a particular dilemma, it is highly likely that it will bring you into conflict with the principal. It may also impact on their family, staff members and CP colleagues. It often takes a strongly committed individual to make difficult decisions and stand by them, but as I alluded to in my introduction to the book, it is one of the ways to make you a cut above the rest and a truly *'Professional'* CPO.

8 GOLDEN RULES OF CLOSE PROTECTION

In Close Protection it is impossible to detail all the rules, regulations, competencies, competences, direction, guidance, techniques, drills, issues, procedures, processes and structures to guarantee an individual is a successful Close Protection Operative. However, based on my broad knowledge and experience, this Chapter should be viewed as a 'one-stop shop' to give you some instant CP guidance to prevent you from making the most common mistakes. By following these rules, you are likely to secure a job, keep a job and impress the principal and everyone you come into contact with. The rules are:

- Always be punctual (NB At least 15 minutes early)
- Be immaculately and appropriately dressed
- Do not out-dress the principal
- Always maintain the highest standards of personal hygiene
- Be tactful and diplomatic
- Maintain a calm and confident temperament
- Be professional at all times
- Remember you are a Close Protection Operative, not a servant
- Blend in and be anonymous as the grey man or woman
- If you think you are in the wrong place, you probably are
- If you think you have said the wrong thing, you probably have
- Give the principal space whenever possible
- Generally, speak when spoken to
- Silence is golden
- Don't lie, be honest and don't waffle
- Don't make idle and silly conversation
- Don't overtly 'listen' to private conversations
- Practice a no news is good news policy
- Be prepared, or you must be prepared to fail

- Be forward thinking - one step ahead of the game
- Time spent on reconnaissance is never wasted
- Always be prepared to communicate, negotiate and compromise
- Practice empathetic assertiveness
- Generally, if the principal leaves late, then they arrive late
- Be assertive and decisive when necessary
- Be prepared to justify decisions
- No crude jokes or inappropriate humour with the principal or staff
- No swearing
- Do not lose your temper as you instantly lose the argument
- Avoid the over-familiarity trap
- Always maintain a professional relationship with the principal
- Try to avoid discussing politics and religion
- Don't drink alcohol on duty
- Go to the toilet when you can, and not when you want to
- Do not smoke on duty
- Do not chew gum on duty
- Relax, or if you cannot relax - Look like you are relaxed!
- Be yourself
- Enjoy the job

9 CONCLUSION

In this publication I have deliberately steered the more popular emphasis of CP away from the reactive unintelligent bodyguard type, to the pro-active thinking Close Protection Operative. As you will now be well aware I am passionate about enhancing professional standards in the close protection sector, and in particular emphasising the importance of the more subtle softer skills of the role. It is no coincidence that the Security Industry Authority Specification for Core Competency Training and Qualifications for the Close Protection Operatives published in November 2004, highlights the importance of communication in their mandatory training sessions. Session 6 is specifically titled 'Interpersonal Skills' and Session 15 is titled 'Communication and Conflict Management Skills'.

The emphasis on communication as a crucial and integral part of close protection is long overdue. Even in the much over-hyped arena of carrying firearms, the guidelines to the police are that they should only be used as a last resort. Other methods must have been tried and failed, or must, because of the circumstances be unlikely to succeed if tried. In simple terms, this means that whenever possible attempts to 'talk' the problem down or oral warnings must be given before a firearm is used as a means of defence. The acknowledgement of communication as a first port-of-call for both conflict management and firearms, is yet further evidence to support my views about the importance of softer skills in CP.

In choosing interpersonal communication skills to be the main subject of my first venture into the world of writing books, I wanted to put an alternative view from the normal type of CP literature. After completing this manuscript I am sure that some people in the close protection sector will conclude that the contents are just a narrow view of a very broad subject. I do not advocate that it is the definitive guide to close protection, and it must be read in conjunction with other publications on the subject. It should be viewed as a book that supports the realities of the operational CP role, rather than the sensationalised gung-ho nonsense that is the subject of so many other publications.

To my knowledge this is the first time that the real importance of the CP softer skills has been documented in such a way. I am content that the subject has now been fully aired, and I would hope that you will approach the professional CPO role with a much more open mind.

The days of the thug-like individual undertaking the bodyguard role will never go away, but it is undoubtedly in decline. The advent of the pro-active thinking CPO is very much in the ascendancy. The mandatory SIA CP licensing system is not perfect, but provided it is policed effectively it will have a positive and profound effect on the future provision of professional close protection services provided throughout England and Wales. There will also be a rippling effect of CP licensing throughout the rest of the UK and to certain extent internationally. Holders of an SIA CP licence will be viewed by both clients and principals with less suspicion, and interpreted as an indicator of a more formally trained complete professional. I am confident that the promotion of much higher standards of CP training and the improvement of individual protective knowledge and skills will ultimately lead to a more professional UK close protection sector.

ILLUSTRATIONS

GLOSSARY

A1 Branch	Metropolitan Police Royalty Protection (Personal)
AAL	Anubis Associates Limited
AFO	Authorised Firearms Officer
BCUC	Buckinghamshire Chilterns University College
CEO	Chief Executive Officer
Client	The employer who pays for the close protection service
CP	Close Protection
CPD	Continuing Professional Development
CPG	Close Protection Group
CPO	Close Protection Officer or Close Protection Operative
CV	Curriculum Vitae
DS	Directing Staff
HM	Her Majesty
HMS	Her Majesty's Ship
HRH	His Royal Highness
MPCC	Metropolitan Police Cadet Corps
MPD	Metropolitan Police District
MPS	Metropolitan Police Service
MVO	Member of the Royal Victorian Order
NVC	Non-Verbal Communication
PPO	Personal Protection Officer / Operative
Principal	The Protected Person
PSI	Private Security Industry
Recce	Abbreviation of the word 'Reconnaissance'
RN	Royal Navy
RST	Residence Security Team
RTA	Road Traffic Accident
SAP	Security Advance Party
SIA	Security Industry Authority
SO14 (2) Branch	Metropolitan Police Royalty Protection (Personal)
TL	Team Leader
UK	United Kingdom
VIP	Very Important Person

WEBSITES

www.anubisltd.com	Anubis Associates Limited
www.the-sia.org.uk	Security Industry Authority (SIA)
www.bcuc.ac.uk	Buckinghamshire Chilterns University College (BCUC)
www.crowdsafetymanagement.co.uk	BCUC Centre for Crowd Safety and Security Studies (Close Protection)
www.etnow.com	Entertainment Technology Press

ENTERTAINMENT TECHNOLOGY PRESS

FREE SUBSCRIPTION SERVICE

Keeping Up To Date with

Close Protection – The Softer Skills

Entertainment Technology titles are continually up-dated, and all major changes and additions are listed in date order in the relevant dedicated area of the publisher's website. Simply go to the front page of www.etnow.com and click on the BOOKS button. From there you can locate the title and be connected through to the latest information and services related to the publication.

The author of the title welcomes comments and suggestions about the book and can be contacted by email at: GeoffreyPadgham@btinternet.com

Titles Published by Entertainment Technology Press

ABC of Theatre Jargon *Francis Reid* **£9.95** ISBN 1904031099
This glossary of theatrical terminology explains the common words and phrases that are used in normal conversation between actors, directors, designers, technicians and managers.

Aluminium Structures in the Entertainment Industry *Peter Hind* **£24.95** ISBN 1904031064
Aluminium Structures in the Entertainment Industry aims to educate the reader in all aspects of the design and safe usage of temporary and permanent aluminium structures specific to the entertainment industry – such as roof structures, PA towers, temporary staging, etc.

Autocad – A Handbook for Theatre Users *David Ripley* **£24.95** ISBN 1904031315
From 'Setting Up' to 'Drawing in Three Dimensions' via 'Drawings Within Drawings', this compact and fully illustrated guide to AutoCAD covers everything from the basics to full colour rendering and remote plotting.

Basics – A Beginner's Guide to Lighting Design *Peter Coleman* **£9.95** ISBN 1904031412
The fourth in the author's 'Basics' series, this title covers the subject area in four main sections: The Concept, Practical Matters, Related Issues and The Design Into Practice. In an area that is difficult to be difinitive, there are several things that cross all the boundaries of all lighting design and it's these areas that the author seeks to help with.

Basics – A Beginner's Guide to Special Effects *Peter Coleman* **£9.95** ISBN 1904031331
This title introduces newcomers to the world of special effects. It describes all types of special effects including pyrotechnic, smoke and lighting effects, projections, noise machines, etc. It places emphasis on the safe storage, handling and use of pyrotechnics.

Basics – A Beginner's Guide to Stage Lighting *Peter Coleman* **£9.95** ISBN 190403120X
This title does what it says: it introduces newcomers to the world of stage lighting. It will not teach the reader the art of lighting design, but will teach beginners much about the 'nuts and bolts' of stage lighting.

Basics – A Beginner's Guide to Stage Sound *Peter Coleman* **£9.95** ISBN 1904031277
This title does what it says: it introduces newcomers to the world of stage sound. It will not teach the reader the art of sound design, but will teach beginners much about the background to sound reproduction in a theatrical environment.

Building Better Theaters *Michael Mell* **£16.95** 1904031404
A title within our Consultancy Series, this book describes the process of designing a theater, from the initial decision to build through to opening night. Michael Mell's book provides a step-by-step guide to the design and construction of performing arts facilities. Chapters discuss: assembling your team, selecting an architect, different construction methods, the architectural design process, construction of the theater, theatrical systems and equipment, the stage, backstage, the auditorium, ADA requirements and the lobby. Each chapter clearly describes what to expect and how to avoid surprises. It is a must-read for architects, planners, performing arts groups, educators and anyone who may be considering building or renovating a theater.

A Comparative Study of Crowd Behaviour at Two Major Music Events
Chris Kemp, Iain Hill, Mick Upton **£7.95** ISBN 1904031250
A compilation of the findings of reports made at two major live music concerts, and in particular crowd behaviour, which is followed from ingress to egress.

Copenhagen Opera House *Richard Brett and John Offord* **£32.00** ISBN 1904031420
Completed in a little over three years, the Copenhagen Opera House opened with a royal gala performance on 15th January 2005. Built on a spacious brown-field site, the building is a landmark venue and this book provides the complete technical background story to an opera house set to become a benchmark for future design and planning. Sixteen chapters by relevant experts involved with the project cover everything from the planning of the auditorium and studio stage, the stage engineering, stage lighting and control and architectural lighting through to acoustic design and sound technology plus technical summaries.

Electrical Safety for Live Events *Marco van Beek* **£16.95** ISBN 1904031285
This title covers electrical safety regulations and good pracitise pertinent to the entertainment industries and includes some basic electrical theory as well as clarifying the "do's and don't's" of working with electricity.

The Exeter Theatre Fire *David Anderson* **£24.95** ISBN 1904031137
This title is a fascinating insight into the events that led up to the disaster at the Theatre Royal, Exeter, on the night of September 5th 1887. The book details what went wrong, and the lessons that were learned from the event.

Fading Light – A Year in Retirement *Francis Reid* **£14.95** ISBN 1904031358
Francis Reid, the lighting industry's favourite author, describes a full year in retirement. "Old age is much more fun than I expected," he says. Fading Light describes visits and experiences to the author's favourite theatres and opera houses, places of relaxation and re-visits to scholarly intitutions.

Focus on Lighting Technology *Richard Cadena* **£17.95** ISBN 1904031145
This concise work unravels the mechanics behind modern performance lighting and appeals to designers and technicians alike. Packed with clear, easy-to-read diagrams, the book provides excellent explanations behind the technology of performance lighting.

Health and Safety Aspects in the Live Music Industry *Chris Kemp, Iain Hill* **£30.00** ISBN 1904031226
This title includes chapters on various safety aspects of live event production and is written by specialists in their particular areas of expertise.

Health and Safety Management in the Live Music and Events Industry *Chris Hannam* **£25.95** ISBN 1904031307
This title covers the health and safety regulations and their application regarding all aspects of staging live entertainment events, and is an invaluable manual for production managers and event organisers.

Hearing the Light – 50 Years Backstage *Francis Reid* **£24.95** ISBN 1904031188
This highly enjoyable memoir delves deeply into the theatricality of the industry. The author's almost fanatical interest in opera, his formative period as lighting designer at Glyndebourne and his experiences as a theatre administrator, writer and teacher make for a broad and unique background.

An Introduction to Rigging in the Entertainment Industry *Chris Higgs* **£24.95**
ISBN 1904031129
This book is a practical guide to rigging techniques and practices and also thoroughly covers safety issues and discusses the implications of working within recommended guidelines and regulations.

Let There be Light – Entertainment Lighting Software Pioneers in Interview
Robert Bell **£32.00** ISBN 1904031242
Robert Bell interviews a distinguished group of software engineers working on entertainment lighting ideas and products.

Lighting for Roméo and Juliette *John Offord* **£26.95** ISBN 1904031161
John Offord describes the making of the Vienna State Opera production from the lighting designer's viewpoint – from the point where director Jürgen Flimm made his decision not to use scenery or sets and simply employ the expertise of LD Patrick Woodroffe.

Lighting Systems for TV Studios *Nick Mobsby* **£45.00** ISBN 1904031005
Lighting Systems for TV Studios, now in its second edition, is the first book specifically written on the subject and has become the 'standard' resource work for studio planning and design covering the key elements of system design, luminaires, dimming, control, data networks and suspension systems as well as detailing the infrastructure items such as cyclorama, electrical and ventilation. Sensibly TV lighting principles are explained and some history on TV broadcasting, camera technology and the equipment is provided to help set the scene! The second edition includes applications for sine wave and distributed dimming, moving lights, Ethernet and new cool lamp technology.

Lighting Techniques for Theatre-in-the-Round *Jackie Staines* **£24.95**
ISBN 1904031013
Lighting Techniques for Theatre-in-the-Round is a unique reference source for those working on lighting design for theatre-in-the-round for the first time. It is the first title to be published specifically on the subject, it also provides some anecdotes and ideas for more challenging shows, and attempts to blow away some of the myths surrounding lighting in this format.

Lighting the Stage *Francis Reid* **£14.95** ISBN 1904031080
Lighting the Stage discusses the human relationships involved in lighting design – both between people, and between these people and technology. The book is written from a highly personal viewpoint and its 'thinking aloud' approach is one that Francis Reid has used in his writings over the past 30 years.

Model National Standard Conditions *ABTT/DSA/LGLA* **£20.00** ISBN 1904031110
These *Model National Standard Conditions* covers operational matters and complement *The Technical Standards for Places of Entertainment*, which describes the physical requirements for building and maintaining entertainment premises.

Mr Phipps' Theatre *Mark Jones, John Pick* **£17.95** ISBN: 1904031382
Mark Jones and John Pick describe "The Sensational Story of Eastbourne's Royal Hippodrome" – formerly Eastbourne Theatre Royal. An intriguing narrative, the book sets the story against a unique social history of the town. Peter Longman, former director of The Theatres Trust, provides the Foreword.

Pages From Stages *Anthony Field* **£17.95** ISBN 1904031269
Anthony Field explores the changing style of theatres including interior design, exterior
design, ticket and seat prices, and levels of service, while questioning whether the theatre
still exists as a place of entertainment for regular theatre-goers.

Practical Dimming *Nick Mobsby* **£22.95** ISBN 19040313447
This important and easy to read title covers the history of electrical and electronic dimming,
how dimmers work, current dimmer types from around the world, planning of a dimming
system, looking at new sine wave dimming technology and distributed dimming. Integration
of dimming into different performance venues as well as the necessary supporting electrical
systems are fully detailed. Significant levels of information are provided on the many
different forms and costs of potential solutions as well as how to plan specific solutions.
Architectural dimming for the likes of hotels, museums and shopping centres are included.
Practical Dimming is a companion book to Practical DMX and is designed for all involved
in the use, operation and design of dimming systems.

Practical DMX *Nick Mobsby* **£16.95** ISBN 19040313668
In this highly topical and important title the author details the principles of DMX, how to
plan a network, how to choose equipment and cables, with data on products from around
the world, and how to install DMX networks for shows and on a permanently installed
basis. The easy style of the book and the helpful fault finding tips, together with a review of
different DMX testing devices provide an ideal companion for all lighting technicians and
system designers. An introduction to Ethernet and Canbus networks are provided as well
tips on analogue networks and protocol conversion. This title has been recently updated to
include a new chapter on Remote Device Management that became an international standard
in Summer 2006.

Practical Guide to Health and Safety in the Entertainment Industry
Marco van Beek **£14.95** ISBN 1904031048
This book is designed to provide a practical approach to Health and Safety within the Live
Entertainment and Event industry. It gives industry-pertinent examples, and seeks to break
down the myths surrounding Health and Safety.

Production Management *Joe Aveline* **£17.95** ISBN 1904031102
Joe Aveline's book is an in-depth guide to the role of the Production Manager, and includes
real-life practical examples and 'Aveline's Fables' – anecdotes of his experiences with real
messages behind them.

Rigging for Entertainment: Regulations and Practice *Chris Higgs* **£19.95**
ISBN 1904031218
Continuing where he left off with his highly successful *An Introduction to Rigging in
the Entertainment Industry*, Chris Higgs' second title covers the regulations and use of
equipment in greater detail.

Rock Solid Ethernet *Wayne Howell* **£24.95** ISBN 1904031293
Although aimed specifically at specifiers, installers and users of entertainment industry
systems, this book will give the reader a thorough grounding in all aspects of computer
networks, whatever industry they may work in. The inclusion of historical and technical
'sidebars' make for an enjoyable as well as informative read.

Sixty Years of Light Work *Fred Bentham* **£26.95** ISBN 1904031072
This title is an autobiography of one of the great names behind the development of modern stage lighting equipment and techniques.

Sound for the Stage *Patrick Finelli* **£24.95** ISBN 1904031153
Patrick Finelli's thorough manual covering all aspects of live and recorded sound for performance is a complete training course for anyone interested in working in the field of stage sound, and is a must for any student of sound.

Stage Lighting Design in Britain: The Emergence of the Lighting Designer, 1881-1950 *Nigel Morgan* **£17.95** ISBN 190403134X
This book sets out to ascertain the main course of events and the controlling factors that determined the emergence of the theatre lighting designer in Britain, starting with the introduction of incandescent electric light to the stage, and ending at the time of the first public lighting design credits around 1950. The book explores the practitioners, equipment, installations and techniques of lighting design.

Stage Lighting for Theatre Designers *Nigel Morgan* **£17.95** ISBN 1904031196
This is an updated second edition of Nigel Morgan's popular book for students of theatre design – outlining all the techniques of stage lighting design.

Technical Marketing Techniques *David Brooks, Andy Collier, Steve Norman* **£24.95** ISBN 190403103X
Technical Marketing is a novel concept, recently defined and elaborated by the authors of this book, with business-to-business companies competing in fast developing technical product sectors.

Technical Standards for Places of Entertainment *ABTT/DSA* **£30.00** ISBN 1904031056
Technical Standards for Places of Entertainment details the necessary physical standards required for entertainment venues.

Theatre Engineering and Stage Machinery *Toshiro Ogawa* **£30.00** ISBN 9781904031024
Theatre Engineering and Stage Machinery is a unique reference work covering every aspect of theatrical machinery and stage technology in global terms, and across the complete historical spectrum. Revised February 2007.

Theatre Lighting in the Age of Gas *Terence Rees* **£24.95** ISBN 190403117X
Entertainment Technology Press has republished this valuable historic work previously produced by the Society for Theatre Research in 1978. *Theatre Lighting in the Age of Gas* investigates the technological and artistic achievements of theatre lighting engineers from the 1700s to the late Victorian period.

Theatre Space: A Rediscovery Reported *Francis Reid* **£19.95** ISBN 1904031439
In the post-war world of the 1950s and 60s, the format of theatre space became a matter for a debate that aroused passions of an intensity unknown before or since. The proscenium arch was clearly identified as the enemy, accused of forming a barrier to disrupt the relations between the actor and audience. An uneasy fellow-traveller at the time, Francis Reid later recorded his impressions whilst enjoying performances or working in theatres old and new and this book is an important collection of his writings in various theatrical journals from 1969-2001 including his contribution to the Cambridge Guide to the Theatre in 1988. It reports some of the flavour of the period when theatre architecture was rediscovering its past in a search to establish its future.

Theatres of Achievement *John Higgins* **£29.95** ISBN: 1904031374
John Higgins affectionately describes the history of 40 distinguished UK theatres in a personal tribute, each uniquely illustrated by the author. Completing each profile is colour photography by Adrian Eggleston.

Walt Disney Concert Hall – The Backstage Story *Patricia MacKay & Richard Pilbrow* **£28.95** ISBN 1904031234
Spanning the 16-year history of the design and construction of the Walt Disney Concert Hall, this book provides a fresh and detailed behind the scenes story of the design and technology from a variety of viewpoints. This is the first book to reveal the "process" of the design of a concert hall.

Yesterday's Lights – A Revolution Reported *Francis Reid* **£26.95** ISBN 1904031323
Set to help new generations to be aware of where the art and science of theatre lighting is coming from – and stimulate a nostalgia trip for those who lived through the period, Francis Reid's latest book has over 350 pages dedicated to the task, covering the 'revolution' from the fifties through to the present day. Although this is a highly personal account of the development of lighting design and technology and he admits that there are 'gaps', you'd be hard put to find anything of significance missing.

Go to www.etbooks.co.uk for full details of above titles and secure online ordering facilities.